Financial Freedom Framework

Practical Strategies and Tips for Achieving Financial Freedom

Publish By: Alex Knight

© Copyright 2024 Alex Knight

All rights reserved. No part of this book may be reproduced, distributed, or transmitted in any form or by any means, including photocopying, recording, or other electronic or mechanical methods, without the prior written permission of the publisher, except in the case of brief quotations embodied in critical reviews and certain other noncommercial uses permitted by copyright law.

Disclaimer: The information contained in this book is for general information purposes only. The author assumes no responsibility for errors or omissions in the contents. The advice and strategies contained herein may not be suitable for your situation. You should consult with a professional where appropriate. The author shall not be liable for any loss of profit or any other commercial damages, including but not limited to special, incidental, consequential, or other damages.

Table of Contents

Introduction..9
Chapter 1 : Introduction to Financial Literacy...............11
   Definition of Financial Literacy...................................12
   The Role of Financial Literacy in Personal Finance...............15
   Common Myths About Money..17
   The Impact of Financial Literacy on Life Choices...............19
   Empowering Individuals Through Financial Literacy...........21
   Final Insights...25
Chapter 2 : Setting Financial Goals................................27
   Types of Financial Goals..28
      Long-term Goals..28
      Short-term Goals...29
      Financial Independence Goals..................................30
      Lifestyle Enhancement Goals...................................31
   Short-term vs Long-term Goals....................................31
   SMART Goals Framework..35
   Tracking Progress Towards Goals..................................38
   Balancing Financial Goals with Personal Values..................42
   Summary and Reflections..45
Chapter 3 Budgeting for Success......................................47
   Steps to create a budget...48

Setting Financial Goals..52
Common Budgeting Methods...55
Tools and Apps for Budgeting..58
Adjusting Your Budget Over Time..61
Final Thoughts...64

Chapter 4 : The Power of Saving..67
Emergency Funds..68
High-Yield Savings Accounts..71
Automated Savings Plans..74
Setting Up Sinking Funds..77
Financial Stability through Strategic Planning........................80
Bringing It All Together...84

Chapter 5 : Investing for Beginners....................................87
Understanding Risk and Return...88
    Risk Tolerance Assessment..89
Different Types of Investments...91
The Time Value of Money..94
Diversification Strategies...97
    Understanding Diversification...98
    Asset Allocation...98
    Rebalancing..99
    Sector Diversification...99
    Geographical Diversification..99

Practical Examples of Diversified Portfolios.....................100
Managing Specific Risks..100
Balancing Risk and Return...101
Avoiding Over-Diversification..101
Conclusion...101

Building a Strong Portfolio..101
Understand Your Financial Goals...................................102
Diversification: The Cornerstone of a Resilient Portfolio
....102
Regular Portfolio Review and Rebalancing......................103
Risk Management Techniques.......................................103
Dividend-Paying Stocks..104
Writing Down Your Investment Strategy........................104
Measuring Performance Against Benchmarks.................105
Seek Professional Advice..105
Emotional Discipline..105
Continuing Education..106

Final Thoughts..106

Chapter 6 : Debt Management Strategies........................107

Types of Debt...108

Debt Repayment Methods..111

Consolidation and Refinancing Options.............................113

Maintaining a Healthy Credit Score...................................116
Credit Score Basics..116
Factors Affecting Credit Score......................................117
Credit Monitoring..118

Credit Building Strategies..119
Financial Planning and Budgeting..120

    Creating a Budget..121
    Emergency Fund..122
    Tracking Expenses...122
    Long-term Financial Goals...123

Final Insights..124

Chapter 7 : Income Streams and Side Hustles...................127

Passive Income Ideas..128

Side Hustle Opportunities...132

Balancing Time and Effort...135

Tax Considerations..139

Evaluating Risks and Returns..142

Final Thoughts..146

Chapter 8 : Planning for Retirement............................147

Understanding Retirement Needs..148

Types of Retirement Accounts..151

    401(k) Plans and IRAs...152
    Roth vs. Traditional IRAs...153
    Other Retirement Vehicles...154

Investment Strategies for Retirement....................................155

The Role of Social Security...158

Long-term Care Planning...162

Final Insights..164

Chapter 9: Insurance and Risk Management..................165

   Types of Insurance (Health, Auto, Home, Life).....................166

   Assessing Your Insurance Needs..170

      Conducting a Personalized Risk Assessment.....................170

      Evaluating Financial Risks and Determining Protection Levels.. 171

      Estimating Asset Values and Calculating Adequate Coverage... 171

      Factoring in Potential Liabilities...172

      Practical Examples and Scenarios.......................................173

      Conclusion..174

   Comparison Shopping for Insurance..174

   Avoiding Common Insurance Pitfalls......................................178

   Key Considerations When Choosing Insurance.....................181

   Concluding Thoughts..184

Chapter 10 : Building Wealth: A Long-Term Perspective...187

   The Power of Compound Interest...188

   Real Estate Investing...191

   Legacy Planning...195

   Continuous Education and Adaptation...................................199

   Maximizing Returns..203

   Final Thoughts...206

conclusion... *209*

   Reference List.. *213*

Alex Knight

Introduction

Imagine being in complete control of your finances, making informed decisions that pave the way for a stable and prosperous future. Picture yourself confidently navigating through the complex world of money management, equipped with the knowledge to secure financial freedom for you and your loved ones. This book is your guide to unlocking the power of financial literacy. It's designed not just as a collection of abstract theories but as a practical manual filled with strategies and real-life examples to help you master money management regardless of your current expertise level.

In today's fast-paced world, financial well-being is a fundamental aspect of daily life. Whether you're a working professional seeking to elevate your financial literacy or someone interested in practical strategies for achieving financial independence, understanding the nuances of money management is non-negotiable. Financial literacy impacts every facet of our lives from the decisions we make about our careers to the way we plan for our retirement. It's an essential skill that everyone needs but few are ever taught.

Financial literacy isn't just about understanding how to save or invest money; it's about developing a comprehensive viewpoint of your financial landscape. It's about debunking common money myths and demonstrating the tangible impact of financial literacy on your life decisions. By enhancing your understanding of personal finance, this book equips you with the tools to navigate the complexities of managing money confidently and wisely.

Imagine the relief of setting realistic and achievable financial goals, the empowerment of mastering budgeting techniques, and the excitement of exploring investment opportunities. You'll learn how to manage debts strategically, ensuring that they don't hinder your financial growth but rather contribute to your long-term success. This book will guide you through income streams, retirement planning, insurance essentials, and wealth-building strategies that promise a holistic approach to financial health.

For example, setting financial goals is often where many begin their journey towards financial literacy. But effective goal setting isn't merely jotting down a wish list; it's a strategic process that includes specific, measurable, achievable, relevant, and time-bound objectives. Through these pages, you'll discover how to define your financial aspirations clearly and create actionable plans to achieve them.

Every chapter is crafted to offer valuable insights, practical tips, and actionable advice that will empower you to take control of your financial present and future. Financial literacy is not just about securing a comfortable lifestyle today; it's about creating lasting prosperity and peace of mind for tomorrow. By the end of this book, you'll have a clear roadmap to financial success, no matter where you currently stand on your financial journey. Get ready to transform your relationship with money and unlock a future of financial freedom.

Chapter 1 : Introduction to Financial Literacy

Understanding financial literacy is the key to gaining control over your finances and unlocking a world of opportunities. It involves grasping basic financial concepts such as budgeting, saving, investing, and managing your personal finances effectively. By equipping yourself with this knowledge, you lay the foundation for making sound financial decisions that can lead to financial freedom and stability. Financial literacy is not just about being able to manage money; it's about empowering yourself to make informed choices that affect your financial future.

In this chapter, we will delve into the fundamental aspects of financial literacy. First, we will define what financial literacy entails and why it is essential for everyone, particularly working professionals and those aiming for financial freedom. We will break down complex financial jargon into understandable terms, so you can confidently engage in financial discussions. Additionally, we will explore the link between financial knowledge and empowerment, emphasizing how understanding financial principles can alleviate stress and improve mental well-being. Through practical guidelines, we will provide steps on creating budgets, building emergency funds, monitoring credit scores, and continuously educating yourself about financial trends. By the end of this chapter, you will be equipped with the tools and knowledge necessary to take charge of your financial well-being.

Definition of Financial Literacy

Financial literacy is the ability to understand and apply fundamental financial skills, including personal financial management, budgeting, and investing. For working professionals and those seeking financial freedom, grasping these concepts is not just beneficial, but crucial for personal financial success. By mastering financial literacy, you equip yourself with the tools necessary to navigate the complex world of finance, making informed decisions that can lead to stability and growth.

Understanding financial terms and jargon plays a pivotal role in achieving financial literacy. The world of finance is replete with terms that might seem daunting at first glance, terms like APR (Annual Percentage Rate), ROI (Return on Investment), or compounding interest. These words are often thrown around in financial discussions, and without proper comprehension, they can create confusion. Simplifying these terms and breaking them down into easier-to-understand language is the first step toward empowerment. For instance, APR is simply the yearly cost of borrowing money, represented as a percentage. Similarly, ROI measures the gain or loss generated on an investment relative to its cost. By demystifying such jargon, we remove barriers that prevent individuals from engaging with their finances confidently.

Highlighting the link between financial knowledge and empowerment underscores why financial literacy is vital. When individuals understand how to manage their money effectively, they gain a significant amount of control over their lives. Financial literacy empowers people to make informed choices about spending, saving, and investing. This empowerment extends beyond personal satisfaction; it impacts one's mental well-being. Knowing that you're making educated financial decisions reduces stress and anxiety related to money matters. For example, understanding how to budget allows you to track expenses and ensure that you're living within your means, which can prevent debt accumulation and provide peace of mind.

Establishing the groundwork for effective money management involves several key principles. One foundational aspect is creating and adhering to a budget. A budget helps you plan your expenses according to your income, ensuring that you allocate funds appropriately across different needs and wants. Another principle is building an emergency fund. Having a reserve of savings for unexpected expenses, such as medical bills or car repairs, ensures that you're financially secure even during unforeseen events. Additionally, understanding the importance of credit scores and how to maintain them can significantly affect your ability to borrow money at favorable rates. Good credit management includes paying bills on time, reducing outstanding debt, and avoiding unnecessary loans.

Guidelines play an essential role in building a strong financial foundation. Here are some practical steps to get started:

1. **Create a Budget:** Outline your monthly income and categorize your expenses. Allocate portions of your income to necessities (rent, utilities), savings, and discretionary spending.
2. **Build an Emergency Fund:** Aim to save three to six months' worth of living expenses in a separate savings account.
3. **Monitor Your Credit Score:** Regularly check your credit report for accuracy and take steps to improve your score if necessary.
4. **Educate Yourself:** Continuously seek knowledge through books, courses, and financial news to stay informed about financial trends and strategies.

Take charge of their financial well-being is another critical aspect. Taking initiative means actively seeking out resources and tools that help you manage and grow your wealth. It could involve attending financial workshops, using budgeting apps, or consulting with a financial advisor. The goal is to foster a mindset where managing money becomes a proactive rather than a reactive process. For example, by setting specific financial goals—such as saving for a down payment on a house, planning for retirement, or paying off student loans. you can create a roadmap for achieving those objectives. Breaking down large goals into smaller, manageable tasks makes the process less overwhelming and more achievable.

The Role of Financial Literacy in Personal Finance

In today's complex financial landscape, financial literacy plays a critical role in shaping personal finance choices. Understanding how financial literacy influences our decisions helps us build a stronger foundation for managing our money efficiently.

Developing key skills for effective financial decision-making begins with understanding basic concepts such as budgeting, saving, and investing. Financial literacy equips individuals with the knowledge to navigate these fundamental principles. For instance, budgeting allows us to track income and expenditures, helping to allocate resources wisely. Savings habits, often underestimated, provide a cushion for emergencies and create opportunities for future investments. Learning about various investment avenues, such as stocks, bonds, and real estate, empowers individuals to diversify their portfolios and achieve long-term financial goals. Knowledge of interest rates, compound interest, and market trends further enhances one's ability to make informed and strategic choices.

Aligning personal goals with financial habits is crucial for achieving success. Setting clear financial goals, whether short-term or long-term, serves as a roadmap. For example, if an individual aims to purchase a house within five years, they need to develop a savings plan that aligns with this objective. This might involve cutting down on non-essential expenses and increasing monthly contributions to a dedicated savings account. Moreover, financial literacy teaches the importance of prioritizing high-interest debt repayment to reduce overall financial burden. Creating realistic budgets that reflect both current financial status and future aspirations enables individuals to adopt disciplined spending habits, ensuring they stay on track towards their goals.

Understanding financial risks and strategies to reduce them is another essential aspect of financial literacy. Risk assessment involves recognizing potential financial pitfalls and learning to mitigate them. For instance, high-risk investments might offer high returns, but they also come with significant potential losses. A well-informed individual knows how to balance their portfolio by including low-risk, stable investments to offset higher risks. Insurance is another crucial tool for risk management. By having adequate health, life, and property insurance, individuals can protect themselves against unforeseen circumstances that could lead to substantial financial setbacks. Emergency funds act as a safety net, providing liquidity in times of crisis and preventing the need for high-interest loans.

Planning for sustainable financial growth necessitates a forward-thinking approach. It involves not only maximizing current earnings but also anticipating future financial needs. Retirement planning is a prime example where financial literacy proves invaluable. Understanding different retirement accounts, such as 401(k)s and IRAs, and their respective tax implications helps individuals make the most out of their retirement savings. Starting early with contributions allows for the benefits of compounding over time, significantly growing one's retirement fund. Additionally, diversifying income streams through side hustles or passive income sources like rental properties can enhance financial stability and growth. Sustainable financial growth also includes regular reviews and adjustments of financial plans to adapt to changing life circumstances and economic conditions.

Common Myths About Money

Dispelling misconceptions that hinder financial understanding is crucial for achieving financial literacy. Many people hold myths and misunderstandings about finance, which can impede their ability to make sound decisions. This section aims to clear up some of these prevalent misconceptions.

To start, let's explore the complexities of the money-happiness correlation. While it is true that having enough money to meet basic needs and provide some comfort can contribute to happiness, the relationship between money and happiness is not straightforward. Studies have shown that beyond a certain point, additional wealth does not significantly increase happiness. Instead, factors such as relationships, health, and personal fulfillment play more substantial roles in long-term happiness. For example, someone earning $75,000 per year may feel just as satisfied with their life as someone earning $200,000 if their other needs and life conditions are comparable.

Moving on, we must challenge common beliefs about wealth and success. Many people equate wealth with success, but this simplistic view overlooks the nuances of what it means to be successful. Success can take various forms, including personal satisfaction, professional accomplishments, and meaningful relationships, none of which inherently require vast riches. Additionally, wealth accumulation often involves significant sacrifices, such as time away from family or personal interests. For instance, an individual who prioritizes career advancement and material wealth might miss out on valuable experiences like spending quality time with loved ones or pursuing hobbies. Thus, reevaluating our definitions of success can lead to a more balanced and fulfilling life.

Next, let's address misjudgments about financial risks. A common misconception is that all risks should be avoided at all costs. However, risk is an inherent part of financial decision-making. The key is to understand and manage risks appropriately. For example, investing in the stock market involves risks, but it also offers opportunities for growth that can significantly outweigh the risks over the long term. On the other hand, avoiding all risk by keeping all money in a savings account may result in missed opportunities for wealth accumulation and the erosion of purchasing power due to inflation. Therefore, it is essential to learn how to assess risk and develop strategies to mitigate it rather than avoiding risk entirely.

Clarifying common misunderstandings about investing is another critical step. Many people believe that investing is only for the wealthy or that it is too complicated for the average person to understand. These misconceptions can prevent individuals from taking advantage of beneficial investment opportunities. In reality, investing can be accessible to everyone with the right knowledge and tools. For example, low-cost index funds offer a simple way for individuals to invest in a diversified portfolio without requiring extensive financial expertise. Additionally, understanding the basics of compound interest and the impact of fees can empower individuals to make more informed investment decisions. By debunking these myths, more people can harness the power of investing to build wealth over time.

The Impact of Financial Literacy on Life Choices

Financial literacy is often confined to the realm of managing one's personal finances, but its reach extends far beyond that. A comprehensive understanding of financial literacy can impact numerous facets of our lives, including relationships, career choices, mental well-being, and even community development. By delving into these connections, we can appreciate how a strong grasp of financial concepts can lead to more fulfilling and stable lives.

First, let's explore the link between finances and personal relationships. Financial stress is a common source of tension in many households and relationships. Disagreements about spending habits, debt management, and financial priorities can lead to conflicts. However, when both parties in a relationship are financially literate, they are better equipped to communicate openly about their financial goals and strategies. This transparency fosters trust and mutual respect. For example, couples who create budgets together and discuss their financial plans regularly are more likely to feel united in their goals and less stressed about financial uncertainties. Essentially, financial literacy provides the tools needed for healthier financial discussions, reducing potential conflicts and enhancing overall relationship satisfaction.

Next, consider how financial knowledge influences career choices. From the outset, understanding basic financial principles can help individuals make informed decisions about their education and career paths. Knowledge about student loans, interest rates, and the long-term cost of educational investments allows students to choose career paths that offer a favorable return on investment. Financially literate individuals are also better at negotiating salaries, benefits, and understanding their worth in the job market. As a result, they're more likely to secure positions that align with their financial goals and lifestyle aspirations. Additionally, those with a strong financial background can better assess job offers, considering factors such as stock options, retirement plans, and other benefits that can significantly impact their long-term financial stability.

Moving on, there's a significant psychological aspect tied to financial literacy. The peace of mind that comes from knowing one's financial status and future is invaluable. Individuals who are confident in their financial skills tend to experience lower levels of stress and anxiety related to money. This confidence stems from having clear strategies for saving, investing, and managing expenses. For instance, having an emergency fund can greatly reduce anxiety during unexpected events like medical emergencies or job loss. Moreover, the sense of control gained through financial literacy boosts self-esteem and promotes a sense of security. People who feel in control of their finances are generally happier and have better mental health compared to those who feel overwhelmed by financial uncertainties.

Finally, financial literacy has a broader societal benefit, positively impacting communities. When individuals understand financial principles, they are more likely to contribute to the economic stability of their communities. Financially literate citizens are better at managing debts, saving for the future, and investing smartly, which leads to a more robust local economy. Moreover, they can participate more effectively in community initiatives, such as local businesses and charities, thereby fostering collective economic growth. For instance, homeowners who understand mortgage terms and property taxes are less likely to face foreclosure, contributing to neighborhood stability and property value retention. On a larger scale, communities with financially literate members tend to have lower rates of poverty and higher levels of civic engagement, as residents feel empowered to make positive changes and advocate for economic policies that benefit everyone.

Empowering Individuals Through Financial Literacy

Achieving financial independence and stability is a goal many aspire to reach. It signifies being able to sustain oneself without relying on others for financial support, providing peace of mind and freedom. This journey starts with proactive financial planning and budgeting, which are critical tools in managing one's finances effectively.

Financial planning begins with setting clear, achievable goals. These goals might include saving for retirement, purchasing a home, or creating an emergency fund. Breaking these larger objectives into smaller, more manageable steps can make the process less daunting. For instance, instead of aiming to save $20,000 in one year, one could target saving $1,667 each month. This approach helps individuals stay focused and motivated, allowing them to track their progress incrementally.

Budgeting is another essential component of financial planning. A well-structured budget allocates income to various expenses, ensuring that essential needs like housing, utilities, and groceries are covered while also setting aside money for savings and discretionary spending. The 50/30/20 rule is a straightforward guideline: allocate 50% of your income to necessities, 30% to wants, and 20% to savings and debt repayment. This method ensures a balance between enjoying life and securing financial health.

Confidence in making informed financial decisions is vital. Many people feel overwhelmed by the sheer amount of options and information available regarding investments, loans, and savings plans. To foster confidence, it's crucial to understand basic financial principles and the ramifications of different financial choices. For instance, before taking out a loan, it's important to evaluate interest rates, loan terms, and one's ability to repay within the stipulated period. Comparing different loan offers and reading the fine print can prevent unfavorable situations and ensure better decision-making.

Continuous financial education is equally important. The financial landscape is ever-evolving, with new investment opportunities, changes in tax laws, and emerging economic trends. Staying informed through reliable sources, such as financial news, books, podcasts, and seminars, can provide valuable insights. Additionally, seeking advice from financial advisors can offer personalized guidance tailored to individual circumstances. Building this knowledge base empowers individuals to navigate their finances with greater understanding and skill.

Another key aspect of achieving financial independence is fostering a sense of control and ownership over one's financial future. This means taking deliberate actions and making conscious decisions rather than reacting passively to financial situations. One effective strategy is regularly reviewing and adjusting financial plans to align with changing life circumstances and goals. For example, if one's income increases, it may be wise to increase savings contributions or pay off existing debts faster.

Moreover, cultivating good financial habits is critical. Simple practices such as tracking daily expenses, avoiding unnecessary debt, and prioritizing high-interest debt repayment can have a significant impact over time. Creating an automated savings plan, where a portion of income is automatically transferred to a savings account, ensures consistent progress towards financial goals without requiring constant attention.

Building an emergency fund is also a cornerstone of financial stability. Unexpected events like medical emergencies, job loss, or urgent home repairs can derail even the best financial plans. An emergency fund acts as a financial safety net, allowing individuals to cover unforeseen expenses without resorting to high-interest loans or depleting long-term savings. Financial experts typically recommend having three to six months' worth of living expenses set aside in easily accessible accounts.

Investing wisely is another pathway to financial independence. While saving money is important, investing allows it to grow over time, harnessing the power of compound interest. Beginners might start with low-risk options such as bonds or index funds and gradually diversify their portfolios as they become more knowledgeable. Understanding risk tolerance and setting realistic expectations are crucial elements of investment strategy. Regularly reviewing investment performance and adjusting strategies as needed can help optimize returns and minimize risks.

Lastly, embracing a mindset of financial responsibility is fundamental. This involves recognizing the long-term impact of financial decisions and avoiding temptations that lead to debt accumulation or impetuous spending. By committing to responsible financial behavior, individuals can pave the way for sustained financial health and independence.

Final Insights

In understanding the fundamentals of financial literacy, we've explored how essential it is to grasp key concepts like budgeting, saving, and investing. This chapter reinforced the importance of demystifying financial jargon and simplifying complex terms to make informed decisions. By learning how to create and adhere to budgets, build emergency funds, and manage credit scores, individuals gain control over their financial lives, reducing stress and fostering mental well-being. These foundational skills are crucial for anyone seeking financial independence and stability.

The journey towards financial empowerment doesn't stop with basic knowledge; it's about actively applying what you've learned. Taking charge of your financial future means continuously educating yourself and staying informed about new trends and strategies. This chapter encourages you to embrace a proactive approach, setting specific financial goals and breaking them into manageable steps. Whether it's attending workshops, using budgeting apps, or consulting advisors, these actions help in making money management a confident and deliberate process. Through these efforts, financial literacy becomes a powerful tool for achieving lo

Alex Knight

Chapter 2 : Setting Financial Goals

Setting financial goals is a critical step in achieving overall financial success. Whether you are looking to buy a home, save for retirement, or simply want to manage your daily expenses better, having clear and achievable financial goals can make a significant difference. Financial goals give direction to your efforts and help you allocate resources more effectively. They also provide a sense of purpose and motivation, encouraging you to maintain financial discipline over the long term. By setting specific targets, you create a roadmap that guides your financial decisions and helps you measure progress.

In this chapter, we will explore various types of financial goals and their importance. You will learn about long-term goals, like saving for a major purchase or retirement, which require sustained effort over many years. We will also discuss short-term goals, such as building an emergency fund or paying off high-interest debt, which can be achieved within a shorter timeframe. Additionally, we will cover financial independence goals aimed at achieving a state where you no longer rely on a regular paycheck. Finally, we will look at lifestyle enhancement goals that focus on improving your quality of life through financial planning. Each section will provide insights and practical tips to help you set and achieve your own financial goals.

Types of Financial Goals

Understanding the different categories of financial goals and how they contribute to overall financial success is vital for anyone looking to improve their financial literacy. In this section, we will delve into various types of financial goals, including long-term goals, short-term goals, financial independence goals, and lifestyle enhancement goals. Each category serves a unique purpose in shaping your financial landscape.

Long-term Goals

Long-term goals are an essential aspect of any financial plan. These goals typically span several years and aim to achieve significant milestones such as buying a home, saving for retirement, or funding a child's education. The importance of these goals lies in their ability to create a roadmap for sustained financial growth and security over time.

For instance, setting a goal to save a certain amount for retirement by the time you reach 65 years old provides a clear target to work towards. It encourages disciplined saving and investing practices that contribute to accumulating wealth gradually. Moreover, the power of compound interest significantly benefits long-term goals. By starting early and consistently contributing to a retirement account, the interest earned on saved money itself starts generating additional income, leading to substantial growth over time.

To set effective long-term goals, it's crucial to be realistic and specific about what you want to achieve. One practical guideline is to follow the SMART criteria: Specific, Measurable, Achievable, Relevant, and Time-bound. This approach ensures that your objectives are clearly defined and attainable within a designated timeframe.

Short-term Goals

While long-term goals paint the big picture, short-term goals focus on immediate or near-future achievements. These objectives usually encompass activities like building an emergency fund, paying off high-interest debts, or saving for a significant purchase within a year.

One key advantage of short-term goals is that they offer quick wins, which can be highly motivating. Accomplishing these smaller objectives builds momentum and fosters a sense of accomplishment. For example, setting a goal to save $1,000 in three months for an emergency fund provides a tangible target. By achieving this, you not only secure a safety net but also build confidence to tackle more extensive financial goals.

A practical guideline for short-term goals is to maintain flexibility. Life is unpredictable, and circumstances can change rapidly. Having the ability to adapt and reassess your goals ensures you remain on track despite potential setbacks. Regularly reviewing and adjusting short-term goals helps keep your financial plan aligned with evolving needs and priorities.

Financial Independence Goals

Financial independence is a significant milestone many aspire to reach. It involves planning for long-term financial stability and security, ultimately allowing you to live comfortably without relying on a steady paycheck. Achieving financial independence requires careful planning, disciplined saving, and strategic investing.

One common goal associated with financial independence is reaching a point where passive income from investments covers all living expenses. This state of financial freedom opens up opportunities to pursue passions, travel, or even retire early. To work towards this goal, allocate a portion of your income to investments like stocks, bonds, real estate, or other assets that generate ongoing returns.

Guidelines for pursuing financial independence include creating a detailed financial plan and regularly monitoring progress. Start by determining your desired level of passive income and calculating how much you need to save and invest to reach that amount. Consistently tracking investments and making informed adjustments based on market conditions will help ensure you stay on course.

Lifestyle Enhancement Goals

Lastly, lifestyle enhancement goals focus on improving your quality of life through financial means. These goals often revolve around personal desires and aspirations, such as upgrading your home, taking luxurious vacations, or investing in hobbies and experiences that bring joy and fulfillment.

It's important to remember that financial planning is not solely about accumulating wealth; it also involves enjoying the fruits of your labor. Setting aside funds for lifestyle enhancements can lead to a more balanced and satisfying life. For example, planning and saving for an annual family vacation creates lasting memories while providing a break from routine stresses.

To achieve lifestyle enhancement goals, prioritize them alongside other financial objectives. Create a separate savings account dedicated to these goals, ensuring you do not dip into funds meant for essential long-term or short-term targets. Setting realistic timelines and budgeting appropriately allows you to enjoy life's pleasures without compromising financial stability.

Short-term vs Long-term Goals

When setting financial goals, it's crucial to differentiate between short-term and long-term goals to ensure an effective plan for the future. Working professionals and individuals eager to achieve financial freedom must recognize the importance of addressing both immediate needs and future aspirations in their financial strategies.

Immediate Focus: Addressing short-term needs and objectives within a shorter time frame is essential for maintaining financial stability. Short-term goals typically cover a period of less than a year and may include tasks such as building an emergency fund, paying off high-interest debt, or saving for a vacation. These goals require a clear action plan and a focused approach. For example, if you're aiming to save $1,000 for an emergency fund within six months, you would need to determine how much money to set aside each month from your income. This straightforward goal allows you to see progress quickly, providing motivation and a sense of accomplishment.

Future Planning: Strategizing for long-term financial security and wealth accumulation is the cornerstone of achieving substantial financial milestones. Long-term goals often span several years or even decades and might include saving for retirement, purchasing a home, or funding children's education. Unlike short-term goals, these require more extensive planning and a commitment to consistent contributions over time. For instance, if you're planning to retire in 30 years, you'll need to estimate the amount required for a comfortable retirement and develop an investment strategy to grow your savings. Diversifying investments, taking advantage of employer-sponsored retirement plans, and minimizing unnecessary expenses are all vital components of long-term financial planning.

Balancing Priorities: Understanding how short-term goals impact long-term financial success is key to creating a balanced financial plan. Short-term and long-term goals are interconnected; success in one area can influence outcomes in the other. For instance, paying off high-interest credit card debt as a short-term goal can free up funds for long-term investments. It's important to prioritize goals based on their urgency and potential impact on your overall financial health. A practical approach might be using the debt snowball method for paying off smaller debts first while still contributing a portion of your income toward long-term savings. Balancing these priorities ensures that you're making progress in multiple areas without neglecting significant aspects of your financial future.

Adaptability: Flexibility in adjusting goals based on changing circumstances and priorities is another critical aspect of successful financial planning. Life events such as job changes, market fluctuations, or unexpected expenses can necessitate adjustments to your financial goals. Being adaptable allows you to respond to these changes without derailing your overall financial strategy. For example, if you receive a significant bonus at work, you might decide to expedite your short-term goal of paying off a car loan, thereby freeing up more resources for long-term savings. On the other hand, if you face a sudden medical expense, you might need to temporarily divert funds from your long-term retirement account to cover the costs. Adaptability ensures that your financial plan remains relevant and achievable, regardless of life's unpredictabilities.

Guideline for Immediate Focus: To address short-term needs effectively, start by listing out specific, measurable objectives. Assess your current financial situation and identify the most pressing needs. Set realistic deadlines for each goal and outline the steps required to achieve them. Regularly monitor your progress and make adjustments as needed. By breaking down larger tasks into manageable actions, you can maintain momentum and stay motivated.

Guideline for Future Planning: Begin by defining clear long-term financial goals aligned with your life aspirations. Calculate the projected costs associated with each goal—such as the total amount required for a comfortable retirement or your child's college tuition. Develop a comprehensive plan that includes saving and investing strategies tailored to your risk tolerance and time horizon. Consider consulting with a financial advisor to optimize your investment portfolio and maximize growth potential. Periodically review your long-term goals to ensure they remain applicable and adjust your plan in response to major life changes or shifts in economic conditions.

Guideline for Balancing Priorities: Create a comprehensive financial plan that integrates both short-term and long-term goals. Start by prioritizing high-impact short-term objectives that lay the groundwork for long-term success, such as eliminating high-interest debt. Allocate a consistent portion of your income toward savings and investments, ensuring a balance between immediate expenditures and future gains. Use budgeting tools to track your spending and identify areas where you can cut back to redirect funds toward essential goals. Regularly reassess your priorities to reflect any changes in your financial situation or personal goals.

Guideline for Adaptability: Establish a flexible financial plan that accommodates unexpected changes and evolving priorities.

Build a buffer into your budget by maintaining an emergency fund to cover unforeseen expenses without disrupting your primary goals. Stay informed about changes in the economic landscape, such as shifts in interest rates or tax laws, that might affect your financial plan. Be prepared to reallocate resources as necessary, whether due to positive developments like increased income or challenges like unexpected medical bills. Review and update your financial goals annually to ensure they continue to align with your current circumstances and long-term vision.

SMART Goals Framework

To set actionable and achievable financial goals, it is crucial to understand the SMART criteria. This method provides a structured framework that ensures your goals are Specific, Measurable, Achievable, Relevant, and Time-bound. By utilizing these criteria, you can create clear paths toward financial success.

Specific Goals form the foundation of the SMART criteria. Without specificity, goals become nebulous dreams with little chance of realization. Consider the difference between "I want to save money" versus "I want to save $5,000 for an emergency fund in the next year." The latter clearly defines what you aim to achieve, making it easier to devise a plan to get there. Being specific about your goals helps focus your efforts and increases your chances of success.

Measurable Targets are the next essential component. Having quantifiable metrics allows you to track progress and stay motivated. For example, if your goal is to reduce debt, specify the amount you plan to pay off monthly. This way, you can monitor your achievements and adjust your strategy as needed. Setting measurable targets also gives you concrete evidence of your progress, which can be highly motivating.

Achievable Outcomes ensure that your goals are realistic and attainable. While it's great to aim high, setting goals that are too ambitious can lead to disappointment and disengagement. For instance, if you're currently saving $200 a month, jumping to $1,000 might not be feasible. Instead, incrementally increasing your savings goal will make it more manageable and likely to succeed. Evaluating your current financial situation and capabilities is vital to setting achievable outcomes.

Relevant Aspirations align your financial goals with your personal values and long-term objectives. It's important to ensure that your goals resonate with what truly matters to you. If travel is a passion, saving for a vacation can be more motivating than generic savings. Moreover, relevant goals help maintain focus, as they connect to broader life ambitions and bring a sense of fulfillment. Aligning your aspirations with your core values ensures sustainability and long-term commitment.

Having established what the SMART criteria entail, let's delve deeper into each element with examples and guidelines to illustrate their practical application effectively.

Defining Specific Goals begins with asking pertinent questions: What exactly do I want to accomplish? Why is this goal important? Who is involved? Where is it located? What resources or constraints are involved? Addressing these questions provides clarity and direction. For instance, instead of saying, "I want to invest," specify, "I want to invest $300 monthly in a diversified stock portfolio to grow my retirement fund." This detailed approach transforms vague intentions into actionable plans.

Establishing Measurable Targets involves setting criteria for measuring progress. Consider using benchmarks like percentages, quantities, or timeframes. For example, if your goal is to increase your emergency fund, you could measure progress by aiming to save 15% of your monthly income until you reach your desired amount. Additionally, keeping a financial journal or using budgeting apps can help track these metrics, providing tangible evidence of advancement and areas needing adjustment.

Ensuring Achievable Outcomes requires honestly assessing your financial situation and capabilities. Analyzing past financial behavior can provide insights into what's realistic. For instance, if you consistently save $100 monthly without strain, gradually increasing this amount might be feasible. Set intermediary milestones to gauge progress and make necessary adjustments. Goal attainability often lies in incremental progress rather than drastic changes. Regularly reviewing and updating your goals to reflect changes in income and expenses will help maintain their achievability.

Aligning Relevant Aspirations means connecting your financial goals with your broader life plans and values. Reflect on what genuinely motivates you. If you value education, perhaps saving for advanced courses aligns better than other investments.

Ensuring relevance makes it easier to stay committed. For instance, if your long-term objective is to retire comfortably in a serene location, then setting shorter-term goals such as paying off your mortgage or increasing retirement contributions becomes more meaningful. Relevant goals act as stepping stones towards larger life aspirations.

Integrating these SMART criteria into your financial planning process doesn't just clarify your objectives; it also enhances your ability to track progress, adapt strategies, and ultimately achieve your financial goals. As working professionals or individuals striving for financial freedom, adopting this structured approach can significantly improve your financial literacy and control over personal finances.

Tracking Progress Towards Goals

Implementing tracking methods to monitor and measure advancements towards financial goals is a crucial element in achieving financial success. One of the first steps in this process is conducting regular assessments of your financial progress. Regular assessments involve monitoring your finances on a consistent basis, allowing you to track how well you are doing in relation to your set goals. This can be done through various tools such as spreadsheets, budgeting apps, or even simple pen and paper. The key is consistency—setting aside time each month to review income, expenses, savings, and investments ensures that you stay aware of your financial standing. For working professionals, incorporating this into a monthly routine can help highlight areas for improvement and affirm where you're excelling.

Adapting strategies is an inevitable part of the journey towards financial goals. Life is unpredictable, and so too are our financial circumstances. To stay on course, it's vital to remain flexible and open to adjusting your financial plans. If an unexpected expense arises or your income changes, revisit your financial goals and adjust accordingly. This doesn't mean abandoning your goals but rather realigning them with your current reality. For instance, if a planned promotion at work gets delayed, you might need to temper your savings targets temporarily. Adaptation requires honest self-assessment and sometimes, difficult decisions. However, by being proactive and willing to make adjustments, you ensure that unforeseen challenges don't derail your long-term objectives.

Celebrating milestones is another significant step in maintaining motivation and momentum towards achieving financial goals. Financial success isn't just about reaching the final destination; it's also about recognizing the progress made along the way. Each small achievement, whether it's paying off a credit card, reaching a savings target, or investing in a new asset, deserves acknowledgment. Celebrating these milestones provides a psychological boost, reinforcing positive financial behaviors. It's important to set tangible rewards for these achievements. For instance, treating yourself to a nice dinner or a modest luxury item when you hit a savings milestone can make the experience more rewarding. These celebrations act as reminders of your capabilities and the benefits of diligent financial planning.

Seeking accountability is crucial for staying aligned with your financial goals. Having someone to share your financial aspirations with can significantly enhance your commitment to them. Accountability partners can be friends, family members, or even financial advisors. By discussing your goals and progress with someone else, you introduce a layer of responsibility that might otherwise be absent. An accountability partner can offer support, provide objective feedback, and remind you of your commitments during challenging times. Engaging them regularly, whether through bi-weekly check-ins or monthly reviews, keeps both parties attuned to your financial trajectory. This shared journey not only keeps you accountable but also provides emotional support, making the path to financial success less lonely and more manageable.

Regular assessments require setting up robust tracking mechanisms. Begin by establishing a clear method of documenting all your financial activities. Budgeting apps like Mint or YNAB can simplify this by automatically categorizing transactions and providing real-time updates. Set specific dates each month dedicated to reviewing these records. Look for patterns in your spending habits, identify unnecessary expenditures, and determine whether you're on target to meet your goals. Establish benchmarks for these assessments, such as monthly savings targets or debt reduction percentages, to measure progress accurately. Over time, these regular check-ins become a powerful tool in managing financial health, offering insights that can lead to more informed and deliberate financial decisions.

When adjusting strategies, it is essential to remain focused on your end goals while being adaptable in your approach. Life events like job changes, medical emergencies, or economic shifts may necessitate alterations in your financial plan. Staying flexible means you can recalibrate without losing sight of your long-term objectives. Develop contingency plans that allow for quick pivots when necessary. For example, building an emergency fund can safeguard against unexpected expenses, ensuring they don't derail your primary goals. Also, periodically revisit your goals themselves: Are they still relevant? Do they reflect your current priorities and values? This dynamic approach allows for continuous alignment with your evolving life circumstances, ultimately fostering resilience and sustained progress.

Celebrating milestones involves both acknowledging the effort put in and recognizing the achievement itself. Start by breaking down your main financial goals into smaller, more manageable sub-goals. Each of these smaller goals should have clear criteria for what constitutes success. Once achieved, reward yourself in a meaningful but financially responsible way. Positive reinforcement strengthens your determination and serves as a reminder of why these financial goals matter. Additionally, documenting these achievements, either through a financial journal or a digital log, creates a tangible record of your progress. Revisiting these records during tougher times can reignite motivation and provide assurance that continued effort will lead to further accomplishments.

Seeking accountability partners transforms an often solitary task into a collaborative effort. Choose someone who understands your financial aspirations and is committed to helping you achieve them. Arrange regular discussions focusing on your progress, challenges, and any required adjustments in strategy. These sessions can be insightful, providing different perspectives and potentially highlighting blind spots in your planning. Moreover, mutual accountability can benefit both parties involved, creating a reciprocal relationship where both you and your partner push each other towards greater financial discipline and success. Using social platforms or forums dedicated to financial goals can also expand your accountability network, connecting you with a community of like-minded individuals aiming for similar objectives.

Balancing Financial Goals with Personal Values

Setting financial goals is fundamentally about ensuring that they align with your personal values and lifestyle preferences. This alignment not only fosters a deeper connection to your objectives but also ensures that you are more likely to commit to achieving them.

Value alignment is the foundation of setting meaningful financial goals. It begins with introspection, where you consider what truly matters to you. For example, if sustainability and environmental conservation are important to you, you might prioritize spending on eco-friendly products or investments in green technologies.

This way, your financial goals reflect your ethical beliefs, making them more motivating and rewarding.

Next, incorporating personal lifestyle desires into financial planning is crucial. Everyone has unique lifestyle aspirations, whether it's traveling the world, owning a house in the countryside, or maintaining a certain level of comfort. It's essential to acknowledge these desires when setting financial goals. By doing so, you ensure that your financial plan is not just about accumulating wealth but also about enhancing your quality of life. For instance, if you cherish travel, one of your financial goals could be creating a specific savings plan for annual vacations. This approach makes your financial journey enjoyable and aligned with your personal happiness.

As life progresses, personal values and circumstances often evolve, necessitating goal adjustments. What mattered to you in your twenties may not hold the same significance in your forties. Therefore, it's vital to regularly reassess and modify your financial goals to reflect your current priorities. For instance, you might have initially focused on saving for a new car but later realized that investing in education or healthcare is more critical. This adaptability ensures that your financial goals remain relevant and achievable.

Taking a holistic approach to setting financial goals means considering all aspects of your life. Financial planning should not occur in isolation; it must encompass various facets such as career aspirations, family responsibilities, health, and hobbies. For example, if you aim to start a family, your financial goals should include provisions for childcare expenses, education funds, and even parental leaves. Similarly, if you're passionate about a hobby, like painting or playing an instrument, allocate funds for lessons, equipment, and related activities. This comprehensive perspective ensures that financial goals support a well-rounded and fulfilling life.

Incorporating these elements into your financial planning does not require a rigid set of guidelines but rather a flexible framework that adapts to your evolving needs. Start by identifying your core values and how they influence your financial decisions. Write down what matters most to you and how you can integrate those values into your financial goals.

Next, take a close look at your lifestyle preferences. Visualize your ideal life and consider what financial goals will help you achieve it. Are you looking to retire early and lead a laid-back life, or do you want to work longer but enjoy periodic breaks? Knowing your preferences helps shape your financial strategy in a way that's both realistic and satisfying.

Keep in mind that goal adjustment is an ongoing process. Schedule regular check-ins, perhaps annually, to review your financial goals and make necessary modifications. Life events such as marriage, career changes, or the birth of a child can significantly impact your goals. Being proactive about these changes allows you to stay on track and maintain financial stability.

A holistic approach requires integrating your financial goals with other life plans. For instance, if you plan to advance your career, consider the financial implications of further education or networking events. Ensure that your financial goals facilitate your professional growth. Similarly, think about how improving your health through fitness classes or nutritious food plans fits into your budget. The idea is to create a balanced financial plan that supports various dimensions of your life.

Finally, remember that setting financial goals is not about sacrificing enjoyment today for a better tomorrow or vice versa. It's about finding a balance where you can appreciate the present while securing your future. For instance, while saving for retirement is critical, it's equally important to allocate resources for experiences and joys you can relish now. This balanced approach prevents burnout and keeps you motivated to pursue your financial goals.

Summary and Reflections

Setting clear, achievable financial goals plays a vital role in shaping your financial future. The chapter has explored different types of financial goals, including long-term, short-term, financial independence, and lifestyle enhancement goals. Each type serves a distinct purpose, from building an emergency fund to planning for retirement and enhancing your quality of life. By understanding the specific nature of each goal category, you can create a comprehensive plan that accommodates both immediate needs and future aspirations.

Balancing various financial priorities requires a strategic approach where adaptability and continuous reassessment are key. Whether focusing on paying off high-interest debt or investing for long-term growth, maintaining flexibility ensures that your financial plan remains relevant amidst changing circumstances. Regularly tracking progress and celebrating milestones can boost motivation and provide clarity on your financial journey. Ultimately, aligning your financial goals with personal values and lifestyle preferences creates a roadmap that is not only practical but also deeply f

Chapter 3 Budgeting for Success

Budgeting for success begins with creating a practical plan to manage your income and expenses. Having a well-structured budget allows you to gain control over your financial situation and make informed decisions that align with your long-term goals. This chapter will guide you through the essential steps needed to develop an effective budgeting strategy tailored to your needs and aspirations.

In the following sections, you'll explore detailed methods to understand your income and categorize your expenses accurately. You'll learn how to allocate funds purposefully, ensuring every dollar serves a specific role in your financial plan. The chapter also delves into tracking variable expenses to maintain financial discipline and introduces SMART goals for clear and actionable objectives. By adopting these practices, you'll build a robust budget that supports your journey towards financial stability and success.

Steps to create a budget

Creating and maintaining a practical budget is essential for achieving financial stability and reaching your financial goals. This section will provide a step-by-step guide to creating an effective budget that aligns with your financial objectives. By understanding your income and expenses, ensuring purposeful allocation of every dollar, tracking variable expenses, and establishing SMART goals, you can construct a budget that works for you.

Understanding Income and Expenses

The foundation of an effective budget begins with a clear understanding of your income and expenses. Start by identifying all sources of income. This includes not just your primary job earnings but also any side hustles, freelance work, grants, scholarships, financial aid, parental support, or gifts. Calculate your total monthly income to know exactly how much money you have available each month.

Next, categorize your expenses. Expenses are typically divided into two categories: fixed and variable. Fixed expenses include costs that remain constant each month, such as rent, mortgage payments, utilities, insurance, and loan payments. These are non-negotiable and must be covered first when planning your budget.

Variable expenses, on the other hand, fluctuate from month to month. These might include groceries, transportation, entertainment, dining out, and personal care. To accurately budget for these, track your spending for at least one month. Collect receipts, review bank statements, or use a spending tracker app to record every purchase. This will give you a realistic view of where your money goes and help you identify areas where you could potentially cut back *(Budgeting and Personal Financial Planning Skills - MAU, n.d.)*.

Ensuring Purposeful Allocation of Every Dollar

Once you've categorized your income and expenses, the next step is to allocate your income purposefully towards essential expenses and savings goals. Begin by prioritizing your fixed expenses. Ensure that basic necessities such as housing, utilities, and groceries are covered before considering non-essential spending.

To effectively manage your budget, adopt the concept of "assigning every dollar a job." This means allocating a specific amount of money towards each expense category based on your income and priorities. For instance, after covering your fixed expenses, determine how much you need for variable costs like groceries and transportation. Then decide how much can be allocated towards discretionary spending, such as entertainment and dining out. Make sure to include a category for savings in your budget as well. Whether it's saving for an emergency fund, a vacation, or long-term investments, setting aside a portion of your income for savings is crucial in building financial security.

One useful method to ensure purposeful spending is the Zero-Based Budgeting technique, where you allocate every dollar of your income towards a specific expense or savings goal, leaving no untracked spending. This approach promotes intentionality and prevents overspending by ensuring that each dollar is accounted for.

Tracking Variable Expenses

While fixed expenses are relatively easy to predict, variable expenses require more attention due to their fluctuating nature. Tracking variable expenses is key to making informed financial decisions and staying within your budget limits.

Start by keeping a detailed record of your daily expenditures. Use budgeting apps, spreadsheets, or even a simple notebook to log every purchase. This practice helps you identify patterns in your spending habits and highlight areas where you might be able to save. For example, if you notice that a significant portion of your income is spent on dining out, you might consider cooking more meals at home to reduce costs.

Additionally, periodically reviewing your spending records allows you to make necessary adjustments to your budget. If you find that certain variable expenses consistently exceed your allocated amount, you may need to re-evaluate your budget or find ways to cut back in other areas. Regular monitoring ensures that you remain in control of your finances and avoid unnecessary debt.

Establishing SMART Goals

Setting SMART (Specific, Measurable, Achievable, Relevant, Time-bound) goals is fundamental to aligning your budget with your financial aspirations. SMART goals provide clarity and direction, helping you stay focused on what you want to achieve financially.

Specific goals clearly define what you aim to accomplish. Instead of stating, "I want to save money," specify, "I want to save $5,000 for an emergency fund." This clarity helps you understand exactly what you are working towards.

Measurable goals allow you to track your progress. Using the earlier example, setting milestones such as saving $500 each month provides a tangible way to measure your advancement toward your $5,000 goal. This keeps you motivated and aware of your achievements.

Achievable goals are realistic and attainable based on your current financial situation. Setting a goal to save $10,000 in three months might be unrealistic if your income and expenses don't support such aggressive saving. Instead, set a goal that challenges you but remains within reach.

Relevant goals align with your broader financial objectives. Ensure that your goals reflect your priorities and contribute to your overall financial well-being. For instance, if debt repayment is a priority, setting a goal to pay off a specific credit card balance by a particular date would be relevant.

Time-bound goals have a clear deadline, which creates a sense of urgency and commitment. Setting a timeframe for achieving your goals helps you stay disciplined and focused. For example, committing to saving $5,000 within one year gives you a concrete period to work within.

Implementing SMART goals into your budget planning involves breaking down each goal into actionable steps. For instance, if your goal is to build an emergency fund, you might start by setting aside a specific amount each month until you reach your target. Tracking your progress regularly ensures you remain on track and can adjust your budget as needed to achieve your goals.

Setting Financial Goals

Establishing short-term and long-term financial objectives to guide budget planning is an essential step in achieving financial success. By setting clear goals, you create a roadmap that directs your financial decisions and helps maintain focus on what truly matters.

When establishing financial goals, the SMART criteria can be extremely beneficial. SMART goals are Specific, Measurable, Achievable, Relevant, and Time-bound. Setting specific goals means identifying exactly what you want to achieve. For example, instead of saying, "I want to save money," a specific goal would be, "I want to save $5,000 for an emergency fund." Measurable goals allow you to track your progress and stay motivated. If your goal is to pay off $10,000 in debt within two years, you can measure your progress by checking how much debt you pay off each month. Achievable goals should stretch you but remain possible; unrealistic goals can lead to frustration and eventual abandonment. Ensuring your goals are relevant means aligning them with your broader life objectives. Time-bound goals set a deadline, which creates a sense of urgency and prompts regular action.

Incorporating aspirations such as debt repayment or savings milestones into your budget can significantly enhance your long-term financial health. Paying off high-interest debt first is often a practical strategy because it reduces the amount of interest paid over time, freeing up more money for saving and investing. Similarly, setting savings milestones, like building an emergency fund or saving for a down payment on a house, provides specific targets to aim for. These milestones not only offer motivation but also give a clear direction for your budgeting efforts.

Adjusting your budget to accommodate unexpected expenses or income fluctuations is another crucial aspect of effective financial management. Life is unpredictable, and unexpected expenses such as medical emergencies, car repairs, or job loss can disrupt even the most well-planned budgets. One strategy to handle these situations is to establish a contingency fund—money set aside specifically for unforeseen expenses. By allocating a portion of your monthly income to this fund, you'll be better prepared to manage emergencies without derailing your primary financial goals.

Income fluctuations, such as receiving a bonus, getting a raise, or experiencing a decrease in earnings, also require budget adjustments. When your income increases, it's tempting to inflate your lifestyle correspondingly. However, sticking to your original budget and directing the excess income towards savings or debt repayment can accelerate your financial progress. Conversely, a drop in income necessitates immediate budget reevaluation to identify areas where spending can be reduced. This proactive approach ensures that you continue living within your means regardless of financial changes.

Proactively modifying your budget based on evolving financial priorities or unforeseen events is vital for maintaining financial stability. As your life circumstances change, so do your financial priorities. For instance, starting a family, buying a home, or preparing for retirement will alter your financial goals and necessitate budget adjustments. Regularly reviewing and updating your budget allows you to align it with your current needs and objectives.

Conducting periodic budget evaluations is an excellent practice. Monthly or quarterly reviews help identify patterns in your spending and highlight areas where you might be overspending. Such assessments can reveal whether your existing budget remains realistic and effective or if it requires adjustments. For example, if you find that you're consistently overspending on dining out, revisiting this category and setting stricter limits can help bring your budget back in line.

Scenario planning is another useful technique for managing potential financial challenges. By considering various "what-if" scenarios, such as losing a job, facing a major home repair, or experiencing a significant medical expense, you can prepare suitable budget modifications in advance. This preparedness minimizes the impact of financial shocks, making it easier to stay on track with your long-term goals.

Integrating debt repayment and savings milestones into your budget is essential for long-term financial health. When prioritizing debt repayment, focus on high-interest debts like credit cards. Refinancing options or debt consolidation can simplify this process by reducing interest rates and monthly payments, allowing more funds to go towards principal repayment. Savings milestones, such as building an emergency fund, serve as safety nets that provide financial security during unexpected events.

Common Budgeting Methods

Budgeting is a cornerstone of financial health, and understanding various budgeting techniques can help individuals tailor their approach to managing money effectively. This section introduces two popular budgeting methods: Zero-Based Budgeting and the 50/30/20 Rule.

Zero-Based Budgeting involves allocating every dollar of income towards specific categories, ensuring no untracked spending occurs. This technique requires meticulous planning and thorough tracking of all expenses. The primary goal is to have zero dollars left unallocated by the end of the month, meaning each dollar serves a purpose, whether for bills, savings, or discretionary spending. This method suits overspenders and detail-oriented planners alike, as it promotes a high level of financial awareness and discipline. Utilizing tools like budgeting apps can simplify the process, helping users log each expense and ensure adherence to their budget. Sources such as "*GOBankingRates*" emphasize that this strict allocation encourages accountability and reduces the likelihood of unnecessary spending *(The 5 Most Effective Budgeting Methods — and How to Use Them, 2024)*.

The benefits of zero-based budgeting extend beyond simple expense tracking. By forcing individuals to plan where every dollar goes, it promotes intentional spending and saving habits. People become more mindful of their purchases, often questioning the necessity of non-essential items. This heightened awareness can lead to better financial decisions and increased savings over time. Additionally, because this method requires a detailed understanding of monthly expenses and income, it allows for a clearer picture of one's financial standing *(How to Choose the Right Budget System n.d.)*.

However, some people might find the rigorous nature of zero-based budgeting challenging. It demands consistent record-keeping and a high level of commitment, which can be overwhelming. To ease these challenges, individuals can adopt digital solutions such as budgeting apps like YNAB (You Need A Budget) or EveryDollar, which facilitate easy tracking and adjustment of expenses, making the process less cumbersome and more manageable.

Another widely used method is the 50/30/20 Rule, which offers a simplified approach to budgeting by dividing income into three main categories: needs, wants, and savings. Specifically, 50% of after-tax income is allocated to needs, 30% to wants, and 20% to savings. This rule, popularized by Senator Elizabeth Warren, is particularly appealing to those who prefer not to delve into extensive expense tracking yet still want to maintain control over their finances. Needs typically include essentials such as rent, groceries, utilities, and healthcare. Wants encompass non-essential expenditures like dining out, entertainment, and hobbies. Savings cover emergency funds, retirement contributions, and other financial goals *(Taylor, 2024)*.

The simplicity of the 50/30/20 Rule makes it accessible and easy to implement, even for those new to budgeting. It provides a clear framework for balancing essential spending with discretionary expenses, reducing the risk of burnout often associated with more restrictive budgets. As individuals become comfortable with this method, they can adjust the percentages to increase savings or accommodate changing financial priorities. For instance, someone aiming to build a larger emergency fund might allocate 25% to savings instead of 20%.

Despite its advantages, the 50/30/20 Rule isn't without its challenges. Individuals with high debt levels or living in areas with elevated costs of living might find it difficult to fit all their necessary expenses within the allotted 50%. Moreover, the broad categories might lack the granularity required for those needing more precise control over their finances. To address these issues, people can tweak the percentages based on their unique situations and prioritize debt repayment within the "needs" category, ensuring they maintain financial stability while working towards debt reduction.

In summary, both Zero-Based Budgeting and the 50/30/20 Rule offer distinct approaches to managing personal finances, catering to different preferences and financial situations. Zero-Based

Budgeting excels in promoting detailed expense tracking and intentional spending, which can foster disciplined financial habits and clarity in understanding one's financial status. Conversely, the 50/30/20 Rule provides a straightforward and flexible framework, making it suitable for those seeking simplicity and balance between essential and discretionary spending.

Tools and Apps for Budgeting

Budgeting for success in today's digital age can be significantly enhanced by leveraging technology-based solutions. These tools streamline the budgeting process, making it easier to track expenses and monitor financial health. By exploring popular budgeting apps such as Mint, YNAB (You Need A Budget), and Personal Capital, individuals can find automated solutions that cater to their unique budgeting needs and preferences.

Mint is widely recognized for its user-friendly interface and comprehensive features. It allows users to link their bank accounts, credit cards, and bills, providing a holistic view of their financial situation. Mint categorizes transactions automatically, which helps in identifying spending patterns and managing budgets effectively. Additionally, it offers personalized tips for saving money based on the user's spending habits. This app is ideal for those who seek an all-in-one solution for tracking expenses, setting budget goals, and receiving insights into their financial health.

YNAB takes a more proactive approach to budgeting by encouraging users to allocate every dollar of their income towards specific categories. This method, known as zero-based budgeting, promotes intentional spending and helps prevent untracked expenses. YNAB's key feature is its emphasis on teaching users to prioritize their expenses and allocate funds effectively. The app provides educational resources and workshops to help users develop better financial habits. This makes YNAB suitable for individuals who prefer a hands-on approach to managing their finances and are looking to gain deeper insights into their spending behaviors.

Personal Capital stands out by combining budgeting with investment management. While it offers standard budgeting tools like expense tracking and goal setting, its primary focus is on helping users build wealth through investments. Personal Capital provides detailed analytics on investment portfolios and retirement planning, making it a valuable tool for individuals with more complex financial situations. Its dashboard gives an overview of net worth, cash flow, and portfolio performance, helping users make informed decisions about their financial future.

For those who prefer manual budgeting, customizable spreadsheets or templates can be incredibly beneficial. Spreadsheets offer a level of flexibility that many apps cannot match. Users can tailor their budgets to fit their specific needs, adjusting categories and formulas as necessary. This hands-on approach allows for greater control over one's finances and can be particularly useful for those who enjoy working with numbers and data.

One of the main advantages of spreadsheet-based budgeting is its adaptability. Users can create detailed budgets that align with their financial goals and review them regularly to ensure they are on track. Customizable templates, available through programs like Microsoft Excel or Google Sheets, provide a structured yet flexible framework for tracking income and expenses. These templates often come with pre-built formulas that simplify calculations and visual representations of data, such as graphs and charts, which enhance understanding and decision-making.

Another significant benefit of using spreadsheets is the ability to incorporate personal preferences and unique financial circumstances. For example, one can include columns for recurring expenses, savings goals, debt repayment plans, and other financial priorities. This customization ensures that the budget remains relevant and practical, addressing the individual's specific needs and objectives.

In addition to offering flexibility, spreadsheets also facilitate detailed record-keeping. Users can maintain a historical record of their financial activities, allowing them to identify trends and make adjustments as needed. This historical data can be invaluable when reviewing past financial decisions and planning for the future.

While technology-based solutions like budgeting apps offer convenience and automation, the manual method of spreadsheet-based budgeting provides a level of personalization and control that some users may find more effective. Both approaches have their own set of benefits, and the choice ultimately depends on individual preferences and financial goals.

Combining both methods can also be a powerful strategy. For instance, one might use an app like Mint or YNAB for daily expense tracking and high-level monitoring while maintaining a detailed spreadsheet for long-term financial planning and analysis. This hybrid approach leverages the strengths of both tools, ensuring comprehensive financial management.

Adjusting Your Budget Over Time

Periodic budget adjustments are essential for maintaining financial stability and achieving long-term financial goals. We all experience changes in our lives, whether it's a new job, a pay increase, or an unexpected expense. Adjusting your budget to reflect these changes ensures that your financial plan remains effective and relevant. Many individuals find themselves struggling with their finances because they fail to revisit and revise their budgets regularly.

One of the critical steps in ensuring that your budget continues to work for you is by reviewing budget performance regularly. This practice allows you to assess how well you're sticking to your financial plan and identify areas that need improvement. For example, you may notice that you're consistently overspending in particular categories or not saving as much as you'd like. By pinpointing these issues early, you can make the necessary adjustments to avoid financial pitfalls. It's akin to having regular medical check-ups to maintain your health; periodic budget reviews help keep your finances in good shape.

Monthly or quarterly budget reviews are highly recommended. These frequent check-ins give you a detailed overview of your spending habits and financial progress. Monthly reviews can help catch small problems before they become significant issues. On the other hand, quarterly reviews provide a broader perspective and allow for more substantial adjustments. Both approaches are valuable, and combining them can offer a comprehensive strategy for financial management. During these reviews, track your income and expenses meticulously to ensure every dollar is accounted for. This habit forms the backbone of sound financial practice *(O'Neill, 2017)*.

Adapting your budget to align with fluctuating income levels or shifting financial objectives is another crucial aspect of successful budgeting. Your financial situation will likely change over time. For example, receiving a bonus at work, facing unexpected medical bills, or deciding to save for a big purchase in the future. Flexibility in budgeting is vital to accommodate these changes. If your income decreases, reassess your priorities and cut back on non-essential spending. Conversely, if your income increases, allocate additional funds towards savings or paying down debt. Adapting to these changes promptly keeps you on track towards your financial goals and prevents stress and financial strain.

Scenario planning is another strategic approach to budgeting that prepares you for potential financial challenges. This involves creating different budget scenarios based on possible future events, such as losing a job, facing large medical expenses, or planning for retirement. By anticipating these situations, you can develop suitable budget modifications ahead of time. This proactive strategy provides a safety net, allowing you to navigate unforeseen circumstances without jeopardizing your financial stability. For instance, setting aside an emergency fund can cushion the blow of unexpected expenses, providing peace of mind and financial security *(Why Budgeting Is Important (Even If You're Wealthy), n.d.).*

Incorporating scenario planning into your budget reviews helps you to be prepared rather than reactive. Think of it as having multiple routes planned for a road trip; if one path is blocked, you have alternatives to reach your destination without significant delays. Financial experts often recommend keeping a buffer in your budget for unplanned expenses. This buffer acts as an insurance policy, helping you handle emergencies smoothly. Additionally, revisiting these plans periodically ensures they remain relevant to your current financial situation and objectives.

Regularly review and evaluate your budget to embrace flexibility and adaptability. This habit fosters a proactive financial mindset, which is crucial for long-term success. Make room for periodic reassessment of your financial goals and strategies. Doing so allows you to pivot quickly when needed, ensuring your budget supports your evolving needs. It's important to remember that a budget is not a rigid document but a living plan that grows and changes with you. Maintaining this perspective can make the process less daunting and more empowering.

Moreover, keeping your budget aligned with your life goals can serve as a constant reminder of why you're making these financial decisions. Each adjustment brings you closer to your dreams, whether buying a home, traveling, or retiring comfortably. As your life changes, your financial goals may shift. Regularly updating your budget ensures that every dollar spent contributes meaningfully towards your aspirations.

Additionally, incorporating feedback from these reviews and scenario plans into your everyday financial decisions can enhance your overall financial literacy. Understanding your spending patterns, financial strengths, and areas needing improvement equips you with the knowledge to make better choices. This continuous learning loop can significantly improve your ability to manage finances effectively, leading to greater financial independence and freedom.

Final Thoughts

In this chapter, we've explored the essential steps to create and maintain a practical budget. By understanding your income and expenses, you can allocate every dollar purposefully towards essential expenses and savings goals. Tracking variable expenses helps in making informed financial decisions and staying within your budget limits. Additionally, establishing SMART goals ensures that your budget aligns with your broader financial aspirations. These strategies collectively enable you to take control of your finances and work towards financial stability.

Adjusting your budget over time is crucial for addressing changes in income or unexpected expenses. Regular reviews and scenario planning help you stay prepared for various financial situations. Tools and apps like Mint, YNAB, and Personal Capital offer valuable support in managing your budget effectively. Whether you prefer digital solutions or manual methods like spreadsheets, finding the right approach for your needs enhances your ability to maintain financial health. By implementing these practices, you can achieve both immediate financial security and long-term success.

Alex Knight

Chapter 4 : The Power of Saving

Saving money is a fundamental aspect of achieving financial security. It provides a buffer against unexpected expenses and helps in planning for future goals. Effective saving strategies can make a significant difference in managing finances, especially when aiming to build a safety net that stands the test of time. This chapter explores the power of saving by detailing how various approaches can help you build a robust financial foundation.

Within these pages, you'll discover practical methods for establishing emergency funds, understanding the benefits of high-yield savings accounts, and leveraging automated savings plans. You'll also learn about sinking funds and their role in targeting specific financial goals. Each section will provide clear, actionable advice tailored to working professionals and anyone looking to enhance their financial literacy. By integrating these strategies, you will be better equipped to navigate financial challenges and move closer to achieving financial freedom.

Emergency Funds

Emergency funds play a crucial role in building financial security by providing a safety net against unexpected financial emergencies. The importance of having such a fund cannot be overstated, as it serves to cushion the impact of unforeseen events that can otherwise destabilize your finances.

Firstly, an emergency fund safeguards against various unexpected situations by offering a financial buffer. Whether it's a sudden job loss, urgent medical bills, or major household repairs, these emergencies can disrupt your financial stability. Without an emergency fund, you might find yourself resorting to high-interest loans or credit cards to manage these costs, which could lead to a cycle of debt. According to the 1st United Credit Union, having several months' worth of living expenses saved can help cover necessities during unemployment while seeking new employment *(Four Reasons Emergency Funds Are Important › 1st United Credit Union, n.d.)*. This highlights the value of an emergency fund in maintaining financial health during turbulent times.

Experts generally recommend saving at least 3-6 months' worth of living expenses in an emergency fund. This recommendation stems from the need to ensure you have enough resources to weather significant financial disruptions without compromising your standard of living. For example, if you face a sudden job loss, having savings to cover rent, utilities, groceries, and other essential expenses will provide peace of mind and allow you to focus on finding new employment rather than stressing about immediate financial obligations. Additionally, unexpected medical events can be financially crippling. Healthcare.gov estimates that a three-day hospital stay can cost around $30,000, making it evident why a substantial emergency fund is necessary.

Determining the ideal size for your emergency fund requires careful assessment of your regular expenses and potential financial risks. Regularly evaluating your income and expenditures ensures that your emergency fund remains adequate. If you receive a raise or notice an increase in your monthly expenses, it's wise to revisit and adjust the amount you're saving. This way, your fund reflects your current financial needs. This continual reassessment helps to avoid situations where the fund may fall short during a crisis.

It's essential to maintain discipline in replenishing your emergency fund after each use. Once you've tapped into this reserve to manage a financial emergency, prioritize rebuilding it to its original level. Ensuring your emergency fund is always adequately stocked preserves your financial stability. For example, if you've used part of your emergency savings for a car repair, allocate a portion of your subsequent income specifically to replenish the fund. This practice prevents the depletion of your safety net and prepares you for any future emergencies.

A practical guideline for maintaining and replenishing your emergency fund is to integrate automatic contributions into your budgeting strategy. By setting up automatic transfers from your checking account to your savings account, you can consistently build your emergency fund without having to remember to make manual deposits. This method also minimizes the temptation to spend money meant for your safety net on non-essential purchases.

Establishing an emergency fund is the first step towards financial resilience. It not only safeguards against immediate financial shocks but also contributes to long-term financial well-being. Beyond the apparent benefits, having a readily accessible emergency fund reduces stress and anxiety associated with financial uncertainties. Knowing that you have a backup plan allows you to approach life's challenges with greater confidence and a clearer mind.

Moreover, adherence to the recommended guidelines for managing an emergency fund also instills disciplined financial habits. When you prioritize saving and regularly review your financial status, you become more attuned to your spending patterns and areas where you can cut unnecessary costs. This awareness encourages better financial decision-making and promotes overall fiscal responsibility.

For working professionals looking to enhance their financial literacy and gain control over their personal finances, incorporating the practice of maintaining an emergency fund into their financial planning is pivotal. Likewise, individuals interested in achieving financial freedom will find that building and preserving an emergency fund is a foundational step towards that goal. Starting with smaller, manageable targets and gradually increasing the savings amount can make the process less daunting.

For instance, aiming to save $500 or $1,000 initially before progressing to three to six months' worth of expenses provides attainable milestones and reinforces positive saving behaviors.

Collaborating with financial institutions that offer low- or no-fee liquid savings accounts can further facilitate the building of an emergency fund. Such accounts remove barriers like withdrawal limits or minimum balance requirements, making it easier to access your savings when emergencies occur *(Emergency Savings, n.d.)*.

High-Yield Savings Accounts

High-yield savings accounts are an effective tool for maximizing your savings growth. They offer higher interest rates compared to traditional savings accounts, allowing your money to grow faster over time. These accounts can be especially beneficial for working professionals and individuals interested in enhancing their financial literacy and achieving financial freedom.

One of the primary benefits of high-yield savings accounts is the significantly higher annual percentage yield (APY) they offer. While traditional savings accounts may offer interest rates as low as 0.01% APY, high-yield savings accounts provide rates that can be over 1%, with some accounts reaching around 5% APY *(7 Best High-Yield Online Savings Accounts of December 2021, n.d.)*. This increase in interest means that the money you save can grow exponentially faster. For instance, if you deposit $10,000 into a high-yield account earning 5% APY, you would earn more than

$500 in interest after one year. In contrast, a traditional savings account with an APY of 0.40% would earn only about $40 in the same period.

To take full advantage of high-yield savings accounts, it's essential to compare various options available in the market. Each high-yield account comes with its own set of features and benefits, so selecting the best fit requires thorough research. Important factors to consider include the interest rate offered, any fees associated with the account, minimum balance requirements, and additional features such as online access or mobile apps.

Online banks, credit unions, and nonbank providers often offer some of the best rates and lowest fees compared to traditional brick-and-mortar banks. Many of these institutions allow you to open accounts online without needing to visit a physical branch, providing convenience and accessibility. When evaluating different accounts, be sure to read the fine print to understand any potential charges and ensure that the account meets your financial needs.

Automating deposits into your high-yield savings account is another powerful strategy to maximize returns over time. Setting up automatic transfers from your checking account to your high-yield savings account ensures consistent contributions. This approach not only helps maintain a disciplined saving habit but also leverages the power of compounding interest. By regularly adding to your balance, you'll see your savings grow more significantly. Additionally, automation removes the temptation to spend money that could otherwise be saved, fostering better financial habits.

Understanding the trade-offs between higher returns and any limitations or requirements associated with high-yield savings accounts is crucial. Some high-yield accounts might require a higher minimum opening balance compared to regular savings accounts. Others may limit the number of transactions you can make per month, typically capping withdrawals at six. It's important to consider whether these restrictions align with your financial goals and usage patterns.

Moreover, while high-yield savings accounts offer attractive returns, they may not suit every savings goal. For instance, if you need immediate access to your funds for daily expenses, a checking account might be more appropriate despite its lower interest rates. Conversely, if you have specific long-term savings objectives, such as purchasing a home or funding education, other options like certificates of deposit (CDs) or investment accounts might offer better returns albeit with different risk profiles.

It's also worth noting that the Federal Reserve's policies on interest rates can impact the APYs offered by high-yield savings accounts. As observed in recent times, savings rates have remained relatively steady due to efforts by the Fed to control inflation. However, predicted rate cuts in the future might cause these rates to fluctuate *(7 Best High-Yield Online Savings Accounts of December 2021, n.d.)*. Keeping an eye on market conditions and staying informed about potential rate changes can help you make timely adjustments to your saving strategies.

Alex Knight

Automated Savings Plans

Automated savings plans have become a vital tool in helping individuals foster consistent saving habits. The ease of setting up automatic transfers from checking accounts to savings accounts or investment vehicles ensures that money is regularly saved without requiring manual intervention. This consistency is key to building financial security and can significantly reduce the likelihood of missing contributions due to forgetfulness or other distractions.

One of the greatest benefits of automated savings is the promotion of disciplined saving behavior. When savings are automated, individuals are less likely to spend money earmarked for savings on impulsive purchases. The process removes the temptation by moving funds into savings before one has a chance to spend them. For working professionals with busy schedules, this system offers peace of mind, knowing that they are steadily working towards their financial goals without needing to remember to make transfers manually.

Customizing automated transfers based on specific financial goals can further enhance the effectiveness of an automated savings plan. Tailoring the frequency and amount of these transfers allows individuals to meet diverse objectives such as building an emergency fund, saving for a down payment on a house, or planning for retirement. For example, someone might set up different automated transfers to various accounts: one for short-term goals like vacations or holiday spending, and others for long-term goals like investing in a retirement account. By aligning these transfers with personal financial aspirations, individuals can ensure steady progress towards each unique goal.

Regularly reviewing and adjusting automated contributions is essential for tracking progress and adapting to changing financial circumstances. Life events such as receiving a raise, experiencing a job loss, or incurring unexpected expenses may necessitate changes in savings strategies. Periodically evaluating the amounts and timing of automated transfers helps ensure that savings plans remain aligned with one's current financial situation and goals. For instance, after receiving a salary increase, one might decide to allocate a portion of the additional income to their savings, thereby accelerating their progress toward financial independence.

Flexibility in modifying savings amounts and schedules is another advantage of automated savings plans. Financial needs and priorities can shift over time, requiring adjustments to savings strategies. Being able to easily change the settings of automated transfers enables individuals to respond promptly to new circumstances. For example, if an individual needs to save more aggressively for an upcoming large expense, they can increase their monthly transfer amounts. Conversely, if facing temporary financial hardships, they can reduce the transfer amounts to avoid straining their budget.

An illustrative example of how automated savings plans work involves a professional named Lisa. Lisa is a marketing manager who has multiple financial goals, including saving for a dream vacation, building an emergency fund, and contributing to her retirement account. To achieve these goals, Lisa sets up automated savings transfers every month. She allocates $200 to her vacation savings, $300 to her emergency fund, and $400 to her retirement account. Each of these transfers happens automatically, ensuring consistent savings without requiring her to take any manual actions.

Furthermore, Lisa reviews her automated savings plan every quarter to assess her progress. Upon realizing she received a bonus at work, Lisa decides to increase her emergency fund contributions by $100 per month, ensuring faster growth. Additionally, during a period when her living expenses rise unexpectedly, she temporarily reduces her vacation savings to $100 per month, allowing her to manage her budget more effectively. This flexibility demonstrates the adaptability and resilience that automated savings plans offer, enabling individuals to handle life's financial ups and downs with greater ease.

Evidence supports the effectiveness of automated savings in promoting disciplined savings habits. A study published by the National Bureau of Economic Research found that individuals who utilized automated savings programs saved significantly more compared to those who did not. The research showed that automation helps overcome behavioral hurdles such as procrastination and the tendency to spend available cash, thus reinforcing positive financial behaviors.

To further illustrate the power of automated savings, consider the concept of "paying yourself first." By automating savings contributions, individuals prioritize their financial goals before other expenditures. This approach is akin to treating savings as a non-negotiable bill, which must be paid each month. Such discipline can lead to remarkable outcomes over time, especially when combined with the principles of compound interest, where saved and invested money generates returns, further enhancing the savings corpus.

Setting Up Sinking Funds

Sinking funds are a powerful financial tool that can significantly enhance your ability to save for specific future expenses without disrupting your day-to-day budget. At their core, sinking funds are dedicated savings accounts set aside for particular purposes such as vacations, home repairs, or big purchases. By allocating money into these funds regularly, you ensure that when the time comes to make those expenditures, you have the necessary resources without needing to scramble for funds or incur debt.

The primary advantage of sinking funds is their ability to segment savings for targeted goals. When savings are lumped together in one account, it's easy to lose track of what portion is meant for which expense. By contrast, sinking funds allow you to focus on specific objectives, ensuring that each goal is met systematically. For instance, if you're planning a family vacation that costs $2,000 and you aim to travel in a year, setting aside approximately $167 a month can steadily build up the required amount without tapping into funds meant for other needs. This method provides clarity and control over your financial planning.

Furthermore, sinking funds can be incredibly effective in preventing the disruption of your routine financial activities. Rather than facing a situation where an unexpected repair forces you to divert regular budget allocations or, worse, dip into emergency savings, having a sinking fund dedicated to home repairs can provide a buffer. This approach helps maintain stability in your monthly expenses, making it easier to manage and forecast your finances without constant adjustments.

Prioritization plays a crucial role in effectively managing sinking funds. It is essential to determine which sinking funds are of utmost importance and contribute to them accordingly. For example, mandatory and predictable expenses like annual membership dues should take precedence over discretionary items like a new piece of furniture. Regular contributions to these prioritized sinking funds ensure steady progress toward reaching your set financial milestones. By routinely setting aside a predetermined amount, whether it's weekly, bi-weekly, or monthly, you create a disciplined saving habit that brings you closer to achieving your goals.

One notable benefit of sinking funds is the promotion of disciplined saving practices. Such financial discipline reduces the likelihood of needing sudden budget adjustments. Consider the scenario where you're hit with an unexpected car repair bill; if you've been regularly contributing to a car maintenance sinking fund, covering the expense becomes straightforward. This practice not only reduces financial stress but also negates the need for high-interest borrowing options like credit cards or personal loans. Over time, this contributes to greater financial security and stability.

To maximize the effectiveness of sinking funds, it's important to periodically review and adjust your contributions based on changing circumstances. Life is unpredictable, and your financial priorities may shift. For instance, if you receive a windfall such as a tax refund or bonus, consider allocating a portion to boost your sinking funds. This can expedite reaching your targets or help you address more pressing financial needs. Conversely, if you encounter unexpected expenses early in the year, temporarily redirecting contributions from less critical sinking funds can provide immediate relief while maintaining overall financial health.

Moreover, avoiding overcomplication is key when establishing sinking funds. While it might be tempting to create a separate fund for every conceivable future expense, doing so could overwhelm your financial management efforts. Instead, focus on a few high-priority objectives initially and expand as you become more comfortable with the process. For example, starting with sinking funds for essential areas like home maintenance, car repairs, and major annual fees can lay a solid foundation. As you gain confidence and see the benefits, you can introduce additional funds for non-essential goals, such as a special vacation or a luxury purchase. This incremental approach keeps the strategy manageable and less daunting.

Another strategic aspect involves leveraging tools and features offered by financial institutions to simplify sinking fund management. Many banks now offer customizable savings buckets within a single account, enabling you to allocate funds to different goals without having to open multiple accounts. This functionality can streamline your saving efforts and provide a clear visual representation of your progress towards each target.

Incorporating sinking funds into your budget is a practical way to foster consistent saving habits and achieve specific financial goals. This methodical approach enhances your ability to strategize for both anticipated and planned expenses, ensuring that you remain financially prepared. By assigning money to dedicated savings buckets and sticking to regular contributions, you cultivate a habit of conscientious saving, bolstering long-term financial stability.

For individuals looking to improve their financial literacy and secure their personal finances, understanding and implementing sinking funds can be transformative. It allows for a proactive rather than reactive approach to managing money, reducing reliance on credit and fostering a sense of financial control. Whether you're planning for a significant purchase, anticipating periodic expenses, or simply aiming to avoid financial surprises, sinking funds offer a structured and efficient path to achieving those objectives.

Financial Stability through Strategic Planning

Enhancing financial stability through planned savings and strategic use of various saving methods is crucial for anyone aiming to build a secure financial future. This section explores the importance of establishing different types of savings accounts and funds, the necessity of regularly reviewing and adjusting these strategies, balancing short-term necessities with long-term investments, and integrating a variety of saving techniques to create a robust financial safety net.

Establishing different types of savings accounts and funds is the first step towards catering to both your short-term and long-term financial goals. Short-term savings accounts, such as those set aside for emergencies or specific upcoming expenses, should be easily accessible. High-yield savings accounts are ideal for this purpose, as they offer higher interest rates compared to traditional savings accounts, allowing your money to grow faster while still being liquid. For instance, setting aside money in a high-yield account can help you manage unexpected expenses without dipping into long-term savings.

Long-term savings require a different approach. Accounts like Certificates of Deposit (CDs) or Individual Retirement Accounts (IRAs) lock your money away for longer periods, offering higher returns in exchange for reduced liquidity. Diversifying across these different types of accounts ensures that you have funds available when needed for immediate expenditures while also growing your wealth over time for future needs. By allocating specific amounts to each type of account, you can tailor your saving strategy to match varying objectives, from emergency funds to retirement planning.

Consistently reviewing and adjusting your savings strategies is essential for keeping them aligned with evolving financial conditions and objectives. Financial circumstances tend to change over time due to factors such as job changes, salary increases, or family additions. Regular reviews allow you to assess whether your current strategy is meeting your goals or if adjustments are necessary. For example, if you receive a raise at work, it might be wise to increase contributions to your retirement accounts or high-yield savings accounts. Conversely, during times of financial strain, reallocating funds to more liquid accounts could provide the necessary flexibility.

Balancing immediate savings needs with long-term investment goals fosters overall financial health. It's important not to prioritize one at the expense of the other. Immediate savings needs ensure that you have enough cash on hand for day-to-day expenses and unexpected events. On the other hand, long-term investments are vital for building significant wealth over time, which can fund larger life goals such as buying a home, paying for children's education, or enjoying a comfortable retirement.

To achieve this balance, consider a split-savings plan where a certain percentage of your monthly income is allocated to short-term savings and another portion to long-term investments. A common approach is the 50/30/20 rule: 50% of your income goes towards necessities, 30% towards discretionary spending, and 20% towards savings and debt repayment. This method ensures that you are not neglecting any part of your financial health while staying disciplined in saving regularly.

Integrating various saving techniques, such as emergency funds, high-yield accounts, automated plans, and sinking funds, creates a comprehensive financial safety net. Each of these techniques serves a unique purpose and together, they provide a well-rounded approach to savings.

Emergency funds are perhaps the most critical component of a financial safety net. They act as a buffer against unforeseen expenses like medical bills, car repairs, or sudden job loss. Financial experts recommend having three to six months' worth of living expenses saved in an easily accessible account. This ensures that you can cover your basic needs without incurring debt during emergencies.

High-yield savings accounts are an excellent way to maximize the growth of your emergency fund or other short-term savings. These accounts typically offer significantly higher interest rates than regular savings accounts, helping your money grow faster. It's important to compare different high-yield account options to find the best fit based on interest rates, fees, and accessibility.

Automated savings plans can be a game-changer for consistent saving habits. By automating transfers from your checking account to your savings accounts, you remove the need for manual intervention and ensure that money is saved regularly. You can set up automatic transfers to coincide with your payday, making saving a seamless part of your financial routine. This method also helps combat the temptation to spend money that could be saved instead.

Sinking funds are dedicated savings accounts for specific future expenses, such as vacations, home repairs, or major purchases. By segmenting your savings into different funds, you can focus on achieving specific goals without disrupting your overall budget. For instance, if you know you'll need a new car in the next few years, creating a sinking fund for that purpose allows you to save gradually and avoid taking on debt when the time comes.

Using sinking funds promotes disciplined saving practices by prioritizing and regularly contributing to each fund. This method reduces the need for sudden budget adjustments and enhances long-term financial stability. By assigning specific targets and timelines to sinking funds, you can track your progress and stay motivated to reach your financial milestones.

Bringing It All Together

In this chapter, we have explored various strategies for effective saving to build financial security. We discussed the importance of emergency funds and how they serve as a buffer against unexpected expenses like job loss or medical emergencies. By emphasizing the need to save 3-6 months' worth of living expenses, we highlighted the peace of mind that comes from knowing you have a safety net in place. High-yield savings accounts were also examined, showcasing their potential to grow your savings faster through higher interest rates. Automated savings plans emerged as a useful tool in ensuring consistent contributions towards your financial goals, making saving a seamless part of your routine.

Additionally, we looked at the role of sinking funds in managing specific future expenses, helping you avoid financial disruptions by planning ahead. This approach allows you to allocate resources for distinct goals such as vacations or home repairs systematically. The overall message is clear: disciplined and strategic saving practices are key to achieving both short-term and long-term financial stability. By integrating these varied saving techniques, you can create a robust financial safety net that supports your journey towards financial independence and peace of mind.

Alex Knight

Chapter 5 : Investing for Beginners

Investing for beginners can feel like stepping into a vast, complex world. The sheer number of options and strategies available may seem overwhelming at first glance. However, the key to building a successful investment portfolio lies in understanding fundamental principles that guide decision-making and risk management. This chapter is designed to lay the groundwork by introducing you to core investment concepts, ensuring you have a solid foundation upon which to build your financial future.

The chapter will delve into the relationship between risk and return, an essential aspect every new investor must comprehend. You'll learn how different types of investments, such as stocks, bonds, and mutual funds, vary in their potential risks and rewards. By exploring real-world examples and practical insights, you'll be better equipped to make informed decisions tailored to your individual financial goals and risk tolerance. Additionally, this chapter will cover techniques for assessing your personal risk tolerance and introduce tools that help quantify risk and return, ultimately guiding you towards creating a balanced and diversified investment portfolio.

Alex Knight

Understanding Risk and Return

Understanding the relationship between risk and return is crucial for anyone beginning their investment journey. Every investment carries some level of risk, which in turn dictates the potential return. Simply put, the higher the risk, the higher the potential reward, and conversely, the lower the risk, the lower the potential reward *(Risk & Return: You Can't Have One without the Other | Texas State Securities Board, n.d.).*

To illustrate, consider two different types of companies: a startup and a blue chip company. Investing in a startup might provide substantial returns if the company grows successfully. However, the risk of failure is high, potentially leading to significant losses. On the other hand, investing in a well-established blue chip company typically offers more stability with lower risks, but this also means the potential for enormous gains is limited *(Segal, 2022).*

Understanding this risk-return tradeoff helps investors make informed decisions. For instance, when market conditions shift, such as during a rise in interest rates, investors may choose to move their funds from stocks to bonds. Stocks usually offer higher potential returns but come with greater risks due to price volatility. Bonds, though offering lower returns, are generally more stable and less risky *(Risk & Return: You Can't Have One without the Other | Texas State Securities Board, n.d.).*

Risk Tolerance Assessment

An essential aspect of balancing risk and return is assessing your personal risk tolerance. This means understanding how much risk you can afford to take based on various factors. These factors include the time remaining until retirement, the size of your current portfolio, future earnings potential, your ability to replace lost funds, and the presence of other assets like home equity, pension plans, or insurance policies *(Segal, 2022)*.

For example, a young professional several decades away from retirement might have a higher risk tolerance. They have more time to recover from potential losses and capitalize on long-term growth opportunities. Conversely, someone nearing retirement would likely prefer investments with lower risks to protect their accumulated wealth.

To help quantify risk and return, investors often use specific measures and strategies. Roy's safety-first criterion (SFRatio), for instance, sets a minimum required return for a given level of risk. The investor then chooses the portfolio with the highest SFRatio, maximizing the probability of achieving the desired return.

Another popular tool is the Sharpe ratio, which compares an asset's return to that of a risk-free investment, typically a three-month U.S. Treasury bill. A higher Sharpe ratio indicates better risk-adjusted performance, aiding investors in selecting optimal investments *(Segal, 2022)*.

Creating an investment portfolio aligned with your risk tolerance is vital. Your portfolio should mix diverse assets to maximize returns while minimizing risks. For instance, including low-risk government bonds, moderate-risk rental properties, and high-risk equities can balance out the overall risk level.

Additionally, understanding the concept of real return is essential. Real return accounts for inflation, showing the actual growth of your investment. If your return is 6% annually, but inflation is 3%, your real return is only 3%. This is crucial because ignoring inflation might give you an inflated sense of financial growth, leading to inadequate planning *(Risk & Return: You Can't Have One without the Other | Texas State Securities Board, n.d.).*

Taxes also play a role in your investment returns. Different investments are taxed differently, and understanding these can help optimize your net gains. For example, municipal bonds might offer lower gross returns compared to corporate bonds. However, if municipal bonds are exempt from taxes, they could end up offering higher net returns.

Taking calculated risks doesn't imply hasty decisions. Proper research, strategic planning, and diversification help manage and mitigate risks effectively. Always anticipate potential issues with any investment and have strategies in place to offset them. Concentrating all savings into one or two stocks is risky; diversifying helps minimize such risks *(Risk & Return: You Can't Have One without the Other | Texas State Securities Board, n.d.).*

Different Types of Investments

Investing can be an effective way to build wealth and achieve financial goals. However, for beginners, the multitude of investment options can seem overwhelming. Understanding the various types of investments and their characteristics is crucial to making informed decisions.

One of the most common investment options is stocks. Stocks represent ownership in a company, and by purchasing shares, investors become partial owners of that corporation. Stocks offer the potential for high returns, as the value of the shares can increase significantly if the company performs well. Additionally, some stocks pay dividends, which provide a regular income stream. However, investing in stocks also carries risks, including market volatility and the possibility of losing the entire investment if the company fails. Stocks are suitable for those willing to take on more risk in exchange for potentially higher rewards.

Bonds are another popular investment option, falling under the category of fixed-income securities. When you buy a bond, you are essentially lending money to a government, municipality, or corporation. In return, the issuer pays you periodic interest payments and repays the principal amount at maturity. Bonds are considered safer than stocks, as they provide regular income and have a lower risk of loss. However, bonds generally offer lower returns compared to stocks. They are ideal for conservative investors seeking steady income and lower risk.

Mutual funds are investment vehicles that pool money from multiple investors to purchase a diversified portfolio of stocks, bonds, or other assets. Managed by professional fund managers, mutual funds provide diversification, reducing the risk associated with individual investments. Investors can choose from various types of mutual funds, such as equity funds, bond funds, and balanced funds, depending on their risk tolerance and investment objectives. Mutual funds are suitable for those looking for a hands-off approach and professional management.

Exchange-traded funds (ETFs) are similar to mutual funds but trade on stock exchanges like individual stocks. ETFs offer diversification by holding a basket of assets, such as stocks or bonds, and can be bought and sold throughout the trading day. They often have lower fees compared to mutual funds and provide flexibility for investors to trade at current market prices. ETFs are suitable for both novice and experienced investors who want diversification and cost-efficiency.

Real estate is another investment option that involves purchasing property to generate rental income or profit from the property's appreciation. Real estate can provide a steady income stream and potential tax benefits, but it also requires significant capital and active management. Investing in real estate can be done directly by purchasing physical properties or indirectly through real estate investment trusts (REITs). REITs allow investors to buy shares in a company that owns, operates, or finances income-producing properties, providing a more accessible way to invest in real estate.

Commodities include physical goods such as gold, silver, oil, and agricultural products. Investing in commodities can be a hedge against inflation and economic uncertainty, as their value often rises when other assets decline. Commodities can be purchased directly, through futures contracts, or via commodity-focused ETFs and mutual funds. However, commodity prices can be highly volatile, and investing in them requires knowledge of market dynamics.

Cryptocurrencies have gained popularity as a digital form of currency and a new investment asset class. Cryptocurrencies like Bitcoin and Ethereum operate on blockchain technology and have seen significant price movements. While they offer high growth potential, cryptocurrencies are highly speculative and prone to extreme volatility. Novice investors should exercise caution and consider the risks before investing in cryptocurrencies.

Certificates of Deposit (CDs) are low-risk investments offered by banks and credit unions. When you purchase a CD, you agree to leave your money deposited for a specified term in exchange for a fixed interest rate. CDs are insured by the Federal Deposit Insurance Corporation (FDIC) up to certain limits, making them a safe place to park cash. However, CDs typically offer lower returns compared to other investments and may incur penalties for early withdrawal.

Annuities are insurance products designed to provide a steady income stream in retirement. By purchasing an annuity, you make a lump-sum payment or a series of payments to an insurance company, which then provides regular income payments in the future. Annuities come in various forms, such as fixed, variable, and indexed, each with different features and risks. They can be a useful tool for retirement planning but often come with high fees and complex terms.

Peer-to-peer (P2P) lending allows individuals to lend money directly to borrowers through online platforms. In return, lenders receive interest payments on the loans. P2P lending can provide higher returns compared to traditional savings accounts, but it also carries the risk of borrower default. It's essential to diversify across multiple loans to mitigate this risk.

The Time Value of Money

The time value of money (TVM) is a fundamental principle in finance that states money available today is worth more than the same amount in the future due to its potential earning capacity. This principle is crucial for making informed investment decisions as it helps investors understand the importance of investing now rather than later.

One key aspect of TVM is opportunity cost, which refers to the benefits an individual misses out on when choosing one alternative over another. When you have money today, you can invest it, allowing it to grow through interest or other investment returns. For example, if you receive $1,000 today and invest it at a 5% annual return, you'd have $1,050 after one year. On the contrary, if you choose to receive $1,000 a year from now, you've missed the opportunity to earn that extra $50, illustrating the opportunity cost.

Another factor contributing to the time value of money is inflation. Inflation erodes the purchasing power of money over time, meaning the same amount will likely buy fewer goods and services in the future. For instance, if the inflation rate is 3% per year, $1,000 today would only have the buying power of approximately $970 after one year. This reduction in value underscores why money is worth more in the present than in the future.

Uncertainty is a significant consideration within TVM. Future events are uncertain; there is always a risk associated with receiving money at a later date. Economic downturns, changes in personal circumstances, or other unforeseen events could affect the ability to receive money in the future. This uncertainty adds a premium to the value of money received today versus in the future.

Understanding how to calculate the time value of money involves two primary formulas: the future value (FV) calculation and the present value (PV) calculation. If you know the present value of a sum of money and want to find out its future value after accruing interest, you use the following formula:

$$[FV = PV \times [1 + (i / n)]^{(n \times t)}]$$

Where:

- FV = future value
- PV = present value

- i = interest rate
- n = number of compounding periods per year
- t = number of years

Conversely, if you need to determine the present value of a future sum of money, you would rework the formula as follows:

$$PV = \frac{FV}{[1 + (i/n)]^{(n \times t)}}$$

These formulas allow investors to compare the value between amounts of money received or paid at different times by converting them into equivalent values at a single point in time.

To illustrate this with a practical example, imagine you're evaluating two projects. Project A promises to bring in $2 million in one year, while Project B is expected to generate the same amount in two years. Using a discount rate of 4%, let's calculate the present value for both projects to see which one is more valuable today:

$$PV(\text{Project A}) = \frac{2{,}000{,}000}{[1 + (0.04/1)]^{(1 \times 1)}} = \frac{2{,}000{,}000}{1.04} = 1{,}923{,}077$$

$$PV(\text{Project B}) = \frac{2{,}000{,}000}{[1 + (0.04/1)]^{(1 \times 2)}} = \frac{2{,}000{,}000}{1.0816} = 1{,}849{,}112$$

Based on these calculations, Project A's value today is $1,923,077, while Project B's value is $1,849,112. Hence, Project A is more valuable because it delivers the cash flow sooner, aligning with the TVM principle.

In addition to direct investment scenarios, understanding TVM aids in making everyday financial decisions, such as saving for retirement, buying a house, or planning large purchases. For example, knowing the future value of your current savings can help you determine how much to save monthly to meet your retirement goals.

Time value of money also applies in scenarios like choosing between a lump sum payment or an annuity. Consider winning a lottery where you must choose between a lump sum payout of $1 million today or $1.1 million in yearly installments over ten years. Using TVM principles, you can assess which option yields a higher total value considering factors like personal discount rates and investment opportunities.

Understanding and applying the time value of money concept empowers individuals to make better financial decisions. By appreciating the significance of opportunity cost, inflation, and uncertainty, and through using present and future value calculations, one can weigh various financial options accurately. This principle not only aids in personal finance management but also in broader investment strategies, ensuring optimal decision-making for enhanced financial well-being.

Diversification Strategies

Diversification is a fundamental concept in investment strategies designed to mitigate risk and stabilize returns over time. By spreading investments across different asset classes, industries, and geographical regions, investors can protect their portfolios from substantial losses that may arise due to any single event impacting one type of asset or sector.

Understanding Diversification

Diversification aims to minimize risk by allocating investments in various financial instruments, companies, and sectors. The principle behind diversification is that a portfolio containing a variety of assets will, on average, yield higher long-term returns and reduce the risk of any single asset performing poorly. For example, if you invest solely in technology stocks, a downturn in the tech industry could lead to significant losses. However, if your investments also include healthcare stocks, real estate, and bonds, the poor performance of one sector can be offset by better performance in another.

Asset Allocation

One key technique for diversification is asset allocation, which involves distributing investments among different asset categories such as stocks, bonds, and cash. This approach helps manage risk by balancing more volatile investments with more stable ones. For instance, while stocks generally offer potential for high returns, they also come with higher risk. Bonds, on the other hand, typically provide lower returns but are considered safer. Allocating funds between these assets can create a balanced portfolio that aligns with your risk tolerance and investment goals.

Rebalancing

Rebalancing is another crucial aspect of maintaining a diversified portfolio. Over time, the performance of different assets in your portfolio will vary, causing the original allocation to shift. Regularly rebalancing—adjusting the proportions of assets back to their target allocations—ensures that the portfolio does not become too heavily weighted in one area. For example, if stocks greatly outperform bonds over a period, your initially balanced portfolio may become predominantly composed of stocks, increasing risk. Rebalancing by selling some of the appreciated stocks and buying more bonds can bring your portfolio back to its intended balance.

Sector Diversification

Investing across various sectors within the stock market is another effective diversification strategy. Sectors may include technology, healthcare, consumer goods, energy, and finance, among others. Different sectors perform differently under varying economic conditions; for example, consumer goods might thrive during stable economic times, while energy stocks might perform well when oil prices rise. By holding stocks from multiple sectors, you reduce the risk associated with any one sector's downturn.

Geographical Diversification

Geographical diversification spreads investments across different countries and regions, mitigating risks specific to any single country's economy. Economic cycles, political events, and regulatory changes can significantly impact a country's market. By investing internationally, you gain exposure to growth opportunities in emerging markets and stability from established economies. For example, while the U.S. economy might be experiencing a slowdown, markets in Asia could be thriving. Investing in both regions allows an investor to benefit from growth in one area while potentially offsetting losses in another.

Practical Examples of Diversified Portfolios

A well-diversified portfolio might include large-cap stocks from the U.S., bonds from developed countries, and equities from emerging markets. Additionally, it could contain real estate investment trusts (REITs) for exposure to property markets, and commodities like gold to hedge against inflation. For instance, an investor might allocate 40% to U.S. stocks, 20% to international stocks, 30% to bonds, and 10% to commodities. This spread reduces the reliance on any single asset class's performance and aims to achieve steady, long-term growth.

Managing Specific Risks

Different types of risk can affect your portfolio, including interest rate risk, inflation risk, and individual security risk. Interest rate risk impacts bonds; when rates increase, existing bond values decrease, which can be mitigated by holding bonds of different maturities and from different issuers. Inflation risk, which erodes the purchasing power of money, can be countered by including assets like real estate and commodities that tend to appreciate with inflation. Individual security risk, where one poorly performing stock can drag down a portfolio, can be minimized by avoiding overweight positions and diversifying holdings.

Balancing Risk and Return

Diversification requires finding a balance between risk and return that fits your financial goals and risk tolerance. Investors seeking higher returns must be willing to accept more volatility, while those prioritizing capital preservation might prefer a conservative portfolio with more bonds and fewer stocks. Newly diversified investors should focus on broad-based indices or mutual funds that provide instant diversification without extensive research.

Avoiding Over-Diversification

While diversification is essential, it's important not to over-diversify. Spreading investments too thinly across too many assets can lead to diminishing returns and increased management complexity. Striking a balance is key—the goal is to have enough diversity to reduce risk but not so much that each investment no longer significantly contributes to the portfolio's overall return.

Conclusion

Building a Strong Portfolio

Creating a resilient investment portfolio is crucial for anyone who wants to navigate the financial markets successfully. A resilient portfolio not only withstands market fluctuations but also sets the foundation for long-term financial stability. Here are some strategies to help you build an investment portfolio that can endure through various economic conditions.

Understand Your Financial Goals

Before diving into specific strategies, it's essential to know what you're aiming to achieve with your investments. Are you saving for retirement, building wealth, or funding your children's education? Having a clear understanding of your financial goals will guide your investment decisions and help you stay focused during volatile market periods.

Diversification: The Cornerstone of a Resilient Portfolio

Diversification involves spreading your investments across different asset classes, industries, and geographical regions. This strategy minimizes the impact of poor performance in any one area on your overall portfolio.

Asset Classes: Diversifying across asset classes means investing in stocks, bonds, mutual funds, real estate, and even commodities. Different asset classes often perform differently under the same economic conditions, so diversifying helps reduce risk. For example, while stocks might be performing poorly, bonds could be providing stable returns. (Ashworth, 2023)

Industries and Sectors: Within each asset class, diversify further by investing in various sectors like technology, healthcare, finance, and consumer goods. If one industry faces a downturn, your investments in other sectors can potentially offset the losses.

Geographical Regions: Economic conditions vary by region, so diversifying internationally can offer additional protection. Investing in both emerging markets and developed economies can provide a balanced approach.

Regular Portfolio Review and Rebalancing

Creating a resilient portfolio isn't a one-time task. Market conditions and personal circumstances change, necessitating regular reviews and adjustments to your portfolio. Schedule periodic checkups—monthly, quarterly, or annually—to assess your holdings and make necessary changes.

Rebalancing: Over time, certain investments may grow faster than others, causing your portfolio to become unbalanced. For example, if your stock investments have increased significantly, you might need to sell some shares and invest in other asset classes to maintain your original diversification strategy. Rebalancing helps maintain your target risk level and aligns your portfolio with your financial goals.

Life Changes: Major life events such as marriage, the birth of a child, or nearing retirement may alter your financial goals and risk tolerance. Adjust your portfolio to reflect these changes.

Risk Management Techniques

Even with a diversified portfolio, you can't eliminate risk entirely, but you can manage it effectively using several techniques.

Put Options and Stop-Loss Orders: These financial instruments can help limit potential losses. Put options give you the right to sell a stock at a predetermined price, acting as insurance against significant declines. Stop-loss orders automatically sell a stock once it drops to a particular price, thus capping your losses. (Ashworth, 2023)

Principal-Protected Notes: These are debt instruments that guarantee return of principal at maturity, regardless of how the underlying investments perform. They are typically used to safeguard investments in fixed-income vehicles.

Dividend-Paying Stocks

Including dividend-paying stocks in your portfolio can provide a steady income stream, which can be particularly valuable during market downturns. Dividends can also be reinvested to purchase more shares, compounding your returns over time. Look for companies with a history of consistent and growing dividend payments.

Writing Down Your Investment Strategy

Documenting your investment strategy can serve as a valuable reference point during turbulent times. Write down your financial goals, risk tolerance, diversification strategy, and criteria for buying and selling investments. This written plan can help you stay disciplined and avoid making emotional decisions during market volatility. (Allison, 2022)

Measuring Performance Against Benchmarks

To gauge the effectiveness of your investment strategy, compare your portfolio's performance against relevant benchmarks. Common benchmarks include market indices like the S&P 500 for stocks or the Bloomberg Barclays U.S. Aggregate Bond Index for bonds. Consistently underperforming these benchmarks might indicate the need to reassess your strategy.

Seek Professional Advice

While self-education and planning are vital, consulting a qualified financial advisor can provide additional insights tailored to your unique circumstances. A professional can help you formulate a comprehensive investment plan, review your portfolio periodically, and suggest adjustments based on market conditions and personal objectives.

Emotional Discipline

One of the most challenging aspects of investing is maintaining emotional discipline. During market downturns, the urge to sell off investments to avoid further losses can be overwhelming. Similarly, the fear of missing out (FOMO) during market highs can lead to hasty and ill-advised purchases. Sticking to your written strategy and long-term goals can help mitigate these emotional responses.

Continuing Education

Financial markets are constantly evolving, influenced by economic policies, technological advancements, and global events. Staying informed about these changes can help you make more educated investment decisions. Subscribe to financial news, read books, and consider taking courses to deepen your understanding of investment principles.

Final Thoughts

In this chapter, we explored the fundamental principles and options available to investors. We discussed the essential relationship between risk and return, highlighting how different investments carry various levels of risk and potential rewards. By examining stocks, bonds, mutual funds, real estate, and other investment types, we provided a comprehensive overview that helps you understand which options may align best with your financial goals and risk tolerance.

Moreover, we delved into the crucial concepts of risk tolerance assessment and diversification strategies. Understanding your personal risk tolerance allows you to create a balanced investment portfolio that maximizes returns while minimizing risks. Diversification further protects your investments by spreading them across different asset classes, sectors, and geographical regions. This chapter equips you with the foundational knowledge needed to make informed decisions and build a robust portfolio tailored to your financial aspirations.

Chapter 6 : Debt Management Strategies

Managing debt is a vital aspect of maintaining financial stability. When debts accumulate, they can become overwhelming and challenging to control. Developing a clear strategy for handling various types of debt can significantly improve one's financial wellbeing. Different forms of debt, such as consumer debt, mortgage debt, student loans, and business debt, each have unique characteristics and degrees of impact on financial health. Understanding these distinctions is key to creating effective and tailored strategies for managing debt.

In this chapter, readers will explore a range of practical techniques for managing and eliminating debt. The content delves into various methods of debt repayment, including the Snowball and Avalanche approaches, which offer different psychological and financial benefits. It also covers essential tactics like balancing payments, negotiating with creditors, and understanding consolidation and refinancing options. By implementing these proven strategies, individuals can take positive steps toward achieving financial freedom while maintaining a healthy credit score.

Types of Debt

Understanding the various types of debt and their implications on financial health is crucial for anyone seeking to manage their finances effectively. The different forms of debt each play unique roles in shaping one's financial stability, and appreciating these distinctions helps in crafting personalized strategies for managing and eliminating debt.

Consumer Debt includes a wide range of borrowing that individuals engage in to cover personal expenses. Credit card debt is perhaps the most common form of consumer debt. It entails borrowing money up to a certain limit to make purchases or withdraw cash, with the expectation of paying it back, usually with interest. While credit cards offer convenience and the ability to build credit history when used responsibly, their high-interest rates can lead to substantial debt if not managed properly. Personal loans are another significant aspect of consumer debt. These are typically unsecured loans offered by banks, credit unions, or online lenders that can be used for various purposes like consolidating existing debt, financing home improvements, or covering unexpected expenses. Unlike credit card debt, personal loans often come with fixed interest rates and set repayment terms, which can make them easier to manage. However, taking out multiple personal loans without a clear repayment plan can strain one's financial resources and lead to long-term financial instability.

Mortgage Debt is distinct from other types of consumer debt due to its specific purpose and secured nature. Mortgages are loans taken out to purchase real estate properties, using the property itself as collateral. This means that if the borrower defaults on the loan, the lender has the right to foreclose on and sell the property to recover the outstanding debt. Mortgage debt generally comes with lower interest rates compared to other forms of borrowing because it is secured by a tangible asset. There are various mortgage structures available, including fixed-rate mortgages, where the interest rate remains constant throughout the loan term, and adjustable-rate mortgages, where the rate may fluctuate based on market conditions. The key to managing mortgage debt lies in understanding the terms of the loan agreement and ensuring that monthly payments are affordable within one's budget. Unlike student loans or car loans, mortgage debt is often considered a strategic investment, as real estate can appreciate in value over time, potentially providing financial gains in addition to satisfying housing needs.

Student Loans represent another complex category of debt, particularly in the United States, where higher education costs have risen significantly over recent decades. Student loans can be federal or private. Federal student loans are funded by the government and often come with benefits such as fixed interest rates, income-driven repayment plans, and deferment options during periods of financial hardship. Private student loans, on the other hand, are offered by banks or other financial institutions and usually require a credit check and a cosigner. They tend to have variable interest rates and fewer flexible repayment options.

Understanding the terms and conditions of student loans is critical for effective debt management. For instance, graduates with multiple loans may benefit from consolidation or refinancing options that combine various loans into a single payment plan, potentially lowering interest rates and simplifying the repayment process. Additionally, borrowers should explore forgiveness programs that might be available for those working in public service or specific fields, which can alleviate the burden of student loan debt over time.

Business Debt differs from personal debt in its connection to business operations and its impact on both personal and business financial health. Entrepreneurs often take on business-related debts to start, run, or expand their ventures. These debts can include small business loans, lines of credit, equipment financing, and commercial real estate loans. Small business loans are commonly offered by banks and backed by the U.S. Small Business Administration (SBA), providing favorable terms and lower interest rates. Lines of credit provide businesses with flexible access to funds up to a predetermined limit, allowing them to manage cash flow more effectively. Equipment financing helps companies acquire necessary machinery or technology without a substantial upfront cost, spreading payments over time. It's essential for business owners to differentiate between personal and business finances to protect personal assets from business liabilities. Effective management of business debt requires thorough financial planning, regular monitoring of cash flows, and maintaining a solid credit history for both the business and its owner.

Debt Repayment Methods

Managing debt effectively can substantially enhance financial well-being. This section focuses on several proven methods for paying off debt efficiently, helping readers to regain control over their finances with clear and actionable strategies.

The Snowball Method is a popular debt repayment technique that focuses on paying off the smallest debts first before tackling larger ones. This method involves listing all debts from the smallest to the largest balance, making minimum payments on all except the smallest. By directing any extra funds toward the smallest debt, you eliminate it quickly and then move on to the next smallest. The psychological boost from crossing off debts can create momentum, encouraging continued progress. It's particularly effective for those who benefit from visible signs of achievement, even though it might not be the most cost-efficient in terms of interest paid *(Curtis, 2023)*.

In contrast, the Avalanche Method prioritizes debts with the highest interest rates. This approach involves listing debts by interest rate, from highest to lowest, and making minimum payments on all except the one with the highest rate. Extra funds are directed towards this high-interest debt until it's paid off, then the process repeats with the next highest interest rate debt. The primary benefit of this method is minimizing the total amount of interest paid over time, which can result in significant savings. While it may take longer to see individual debts eliminated compared to the Snowball Method, the overall financial savings can be substantial *(Steinberg & Snider, 2019)*.

Balancing Payments while managing debt is crucial, especially when considering other financial goals and obligations. The key is to develop a budget that accommodates debt repayment without neglecting essential expenses or future financial planning. Begin by identifying all sources of income and categorizing expenses as either fixed or variable. Fixed expenses, such as rent and utilities, must be paid regularly, while variable expenses, like dining out, can often be adjusted. By scrutinizing these categories, individuals can find areas where spending can be reduced. For instance, cutting back on non-essential purchases can free up funds for debt repayment. Integrating savings goals within the budget is also important, ensuring that some funds are allocated towards building an emergency fund or retirement savings. This balanced approach helps maintain financial stability while working towards a debt-free future.

Negotiation Tactics with creditors can play a pivotal role in managing debt more efficiently. Creditors are often willing to negotiate terms, especially if it means avoiding defaults. One effective tactic is to contact creditors directly and discuss the possibility of lowering interest rates or extending payment terms. Demonstrating a genuine commitment to paying off the debt and providing a clear picture of one's financial situation can aid in these negotiations. It's helpful to prepare by gathering all relevant financial information and understanding what terms would be realistically manageable. Another strategy involves seeking professional help from a credit counseling agency. These agencies can mediate negotiations with creditors and offer structured repayment plans, often with reduced interest rates and fees. Additionally, for those struggling with credit card debt, transferring balances to a card with a lower interest rate during a promotional period can reduce the overall interest paid, assuming the debt is paid off before the higher rates resume.

Integrating these methods—Snowball, Avalanche, balancing payments, and negotiation tactics—into a comprehensive debt management plan can significantly improve one's financial health. For example, starting with the Snowball Method might provide initial motivation, allowing quick wins that keep morale high. Once confidence and discipline are established, transitioning to the Avalanche Method can optimize long-term savings on interest. Throughout this process, maintaining a well-balanced budget ensures that essential expenses and savings goals are met, preventing new debt from accumulating.

Consolidation and Refinancing Options

Effective debt management not only involves understanding the amount owed but also seeking ways to streamline this debt and potentially reduce interest rates. By exploring various debt reduction techniques such as debt consolidation loans, balance transfers, refinancing mortgages, and professional debt management plans, individuals can take significant steps toward financial freedom.

Debt Consolidation Loans are a popular option for those juggling multiple debts. This strategy involves combining several debts into one single loan, usually at a lower interest rate. The primary benefit is a simplified repayment process, reducing the hassle of managing multiple payments each month. Instead of keeping track of numerous due dates and varying interest rates, you focus on repaying a single loan. Debt consolidation can lead to lesser monthly payments, freeing up cash flow for other essential expenses or savings. However, it's crucial to secure a loan with a lower interest rate than your current debts; otherwise, you could end up paying more over time. For example, if you have credit card debt with an annual percentage rate (APR) of 20% and you consolidate into a personal loan with an APR of 10%, you'll save substantially on interest payments. It's advisable to consult with a financial advisor to ensure debt consolidation aligns with your financial goals.

Another effective technique is the Balance Transfer method, particularly useful for credit card debt. This involves transferring high-interest credit card balances to a card with a lower interest rate, often one that offers a promotional period with 0% APR. During this promotional period, which typically lasts between 12 to 18 months, any payments made go directly toward the principal balance rather than interest, thereby accelerating debt repayment. It's essential to be aware of balance transfer fees, which generally range from 3% to 5% of the transferred amount. For instance, if you transfer $5,000 with a 3% fee, you'll pay an additional $150. To maximize benefits, strive to pay off the transferred balance before the promotional period ends, as the interest rate may spike afterward.

Refinancing Mortgages is another valuable tool for managing and reducing debt. Refinancing involves replacing your existing mortgage with a new one, ideally at a lower interest rate. A lower interest rate can significantly reduce monthly mortgage payments, freeing up funds for other financial obligations or debt repayments. Additionally, refinancing can help convert an adjustable-rate mortgage to a fixed-rate mortgage, providing predictable monthly payments and shielding against interest rate hikes. For example, if you refinance a $200,000 mortgage from a 5% interest rate to a 3.5% interest rate, you could save thousands of dollars over the life of the loan. Before proceeding, consider the closing costs associated with refinancing, as these can offset potential savings if not factored carefully.

Debt Management Plans (DMPs) involve collaborating with professional credit counseling agencies to create a structured repayment plan tailored to your financial situation. These plans are designed to reduce the interest rates on your debts and allow you to make affordable monthly payments to the counseling agency, which then distributes the payments to your creditors. One of the key advantages of a DMP is the possibility of lowering interest rates and waiving late fees, making the debt more manageable. Enrolling in a DMP might also protect you from creditors' collections actions. For instance, a counselor from a reputable nonprofit organization will negotiate on your behalf to establish a realistic payment schedule. It's important to research and ensure the credit counseling agency is reputable and certified, as there are fees associated with these programs.

Implementing these strategies can have a profound impact not only on streamlining your debt but also on alleviating financial stress. Each method requires careful consideration of the terms and conditions involved, and sometimes professional advice can provide clarity. Consultation from a financial advisor or credit counselor can guide you effectively, ensuring you select a strategy that best suits your financial profile and long-term goals.

Maintaining a Healthy Credit Score

Understanding the importance of a good credit score in debt management and overall financial health is crucial for anyone looking to enhance their financial literacy. Your credit score not only affects your ability to borrow money but also influences the interest rates you will pay on loans and the insurance premiums you may face. A strong credit score can open doors to better financial opportunities, while a poor one can create significant barriers.

Credit Score Basics

A credit score is a numerical representation of your creditworthiness based on previous financial transactions and timely payments on loans, credit card balances, and other debts. It's calculated by credit bureaus using proprietary formulas that take into account various factors such as the number and size of a borrower's loans, credit accounts, the length of time credit has been established, and the amount of new credit (Dean & Nicholas, 2018).

Your credit score typically ranges from 300 to 850. The higher the score, the better your creditworthiness. A score above 700 is generally considered good, while scores over 800 are excellent. On the other end, scores below 600 indicate a higher risk for lenders. Understanding how this score is computed helps in managing it effectively.

Factors Affecting Credit Score

Several key factors influence your credit score:

1. **Payment History**: This is the most significant factor. Consistently paying your bills on time shows that you are reliable and responsible with your finances. Missing payments, even once or twice, can have a substantial negative impact on your score.
2. **Credit Utilization Ratio**: This measures the amount of credit you are using compared to your total available credit. A lower utilization ratio is better. For instance, if you have a total credit limit of $10,000 and you're using $3,000, your credit utilization ratio is 30%. Keeping this ratio below 30%, preferably around 10%, is optimal for maintaining a good score.
3. **Length of Credit History**: The longer your credit history, the better. This includes the age of your oldest account, the age of your newest account, and the average

age of all your accounts. A lengthy credit history provides more data points for lenders to consider.
4. **Types of Credit Used**: Having a mix of different types of credit, such as credit cards, installment loans, and mortgages, can positively impact your score. It shows that you can manage various forms of credit responsibly.
5. **New Credit Inquiries**: Each time you apply for new credit, a hard inquiry is placed on your report. Multiple inquiries within a short period can lower your score. However, these effects are usually temporary and diminish over time.

Improving these factors involves timely bill payments, reducing outstanding debt, avoiding unnecessary credit inquiries, and keeping credit accounts open to extend the length of your credit history.

Credit Monitoring

Regularly monitoring your credit report is essential for maintaining accuracy and preventing identity theft. Credit reports can be obtained annually for free from each of the three major credit bureaus: Experian, TransUnion, and Equifax. Reviewing your report allows you to spot errors or discrepancies that could unfairly lower your score.

Checking your credit report can reveal unauthorized accounts opened in your name, a common sign of identity theft. Early detection enables you to act quickly, freezing accounts and notifying the appropriate authorities to minimize damage.

Additionally, monitoring your report helps ensure that all recorded information is correct and up-to-date, reflecting your true financial behavior.

It's advisable to set up alerts through your bank or credit monitoring services that inform you of any significant changes to your credit report. This proactive approach allows you to handle potential issues before they become bigger problems.

Credit Building Strategies

Building and maintaining a healthy credit profile requires conscientious effort. Here are some strategies to help you along the way:

1. **Timely Payments**: Always pay your bills on time. Setting up automatic payments or reminders ensures you do not miss due dates. Even small unpaid bills can lead to negative marks on your credit report.

2. **Reduce Debt**: Aim to pay down existing debt, particularly revolving debt like credit card balances. Focus on paying off high-interest debt first to reduce the overall cost of borrowing.

3. **Secured Credit Cards**: If you have a limited credit history or past issues, consider a secured credit card. These require a deposit that serves as collateral, making them easier to obtain. Using the card responsibly and paying the balance in full each month can help build your credit score.

4. **Become an Authorized User**: Being added as an authorized user on someone else's credit account, especially if they have a good credit history, can boost your credit score. Ensure that the primary account holder maintains good credit habits.

5. **Limit New Credit Applications**: Avoid opening multiple credit accounts in a short period. Instead, focus on maintaining and managing your current accounts well.

6. **Keep Old Accounts Open**: Unless there are significant fees associated, keep old credit accounts open. They contribute to the length of your credit history and provide additional available credit, which can lower your utilization ratio.

7. **Monitor and Dispute Errors**: Regularly check your credit report for inaccuracies and dispute any errors immediately. Even small errors can negatively affect your score.

Financial Planning and Budgeting

Establishing effective budgeting strategies is paramount for managing debt and preventing future financial stress. By creating a realistic budget, building an emergency fund, tracking expenses, and planning for long-term financial goals, individuals can gain control over their finances and work toward a stable financial future.

Creating a Budget

Creating a budget is the first step in managing debt effectively. A budget helps you understand where your money is going and ensures that you allocate funds toward debt repayment while covering necessary expenses. Here are steps to develop a realistic budget:

1. **Assess Income and Expenses**: Start by determining your net income, which is the amount you take home after taxes and other deductions. Next, list all your fixed expenses such as rent/mortgage, utilities, insurance, and loan payments. Then, account for variable expenses like groceries, transportation, and entertainment.

2. **Set Priorities**: Rank your expenses in order of importance. Essential expenses such as housing, food, and transportation should come first. Allocate funds toward these before considering discretionary spending.

3. **Allocate Funds for Debt Repayment**: Dedicate a portion of your budget specifically for debt repayment. Determine how much you can afford to pay beyond the minimum required payment to accelerate debt reduction and save on interest costs.

4. **Adjust and Monitor**: Since a budget is not static, it's important to regularly review and adjust it. If your income changes or unexpected expenses arise, revise your budget accordingly to stay on track (Budgeting and Personal Financial Planning Skills - MAU, n.d.).

Emergency Fund

An essential part of debt management is building an emergency fund. This fund acts as a financial safety net, enabling you to cover unexpected expenses without accumulating new debt. Here are some guidelines for establishing an emergency fund:

1. **Start Small**: Begin by saving a small, manageable amount each month. For instance, saving $20 per month can gradually build up your emergency fund.

2. **Increase Savings Gradually**: As your financial situation improves, aim to increase your monthly savings. Ideally, your emergency fund should cover three to six months' worth of living expenses.

3. **Keep It Accessible but Separate**: Ensure the emergency fund is easily accessible in case of emergencies but keep it separate from your regular checking account to avoid unnecessary withdrawals.

4. **Use Only for Emergencies**: The fund should only be used for true emergencies, such as medical expenses, car repairs, or job loss. Regular expenses or minor inconveniences shouldn't deplete this reserve (Financial Literacy and Budgeting, n.d.).

Tracking Expenses

Tracking daily expenses is crucial to staying within budget limits. Understanding your spending patterns can help identify areas where you can cut back and allocate more funds toward debt repayment. Here are some techniques for effective expense tracking:

1. **Utilize Budgeting Tools**: Apps like Mint, YNAB (You Need A Budget), and PocketGuard can help you monitor your income and expenses in real-time.

2. **Maintain a Spending Journal**: Keep a daily record of every transaction, no matter how small. This exercise increases awareness of spending habits and highlights unnecessary expenditures.

3. **Categorize Expenses**: Break down your expenses into categories such as food, transportation, entertainment, and personal care. This will make it easier to see where most of your money is going and identify potential savings.

4. **Review Statements**: Regularly review your bank and credit card statements to ensure all charges are accurate and to spot any unusual or unauthorized transactions quickly *(Budgeting and Personal Financial Planning Skills - MAU, n.d.)*.

Long-term Financial Goals

While managing current debt obligations, it is equally important to plan for long-term financial stability. Setting and working toward long-term goals can provide motivation and direction in your financial journey. Here are strategies for planning long-term financial goals:

1. **Define Clear Goals**: Identify what you want to achieve financially in the long run, such as buying a house, starting a business, or saving for retirement. Make sure your goals are specific, measurable, achievable, relevant, and time-bound (SMART).

2. **Create a Plan**: Develop a plan detailing the steps needed to reach your long-term goals. This may include saving a certain percentage of your income, investing in stocks or mutual funds, or paying off high-interest debt first.

3. **Balance Short-term and Long-term Goals**: While focusing on debt repayment, don't neglect saving for future needs. Allocate a portion of your budget to savings and investments that align with your long-term objectives.

4. **Continually Assess Progress**: Regularly review your progress toward long-term goals and make adjustments as needed. Life circumstances and financial markets change, so it's important to stay flexible and adapt your plans accordingly *(Financial Literacy and Budgeting, n.d.)*.

Final Insights

In this chapter, we explored various techniques for managing and eliminating debt. We delved into understanding different types of debt such as consumer debt, mortgage debt, student loans, and business debt, each with its unique features and implications. By recognizing these variations, you can tailor your debt management strategies more effectively. We also covered practical repayment methods like the Snowball and Avalanche methods, balancing payments while budgeting, and negotiation tactics to reduce interest rates or extend payment terms. These strategies provide a structured approach to tackling debt and regaining control over your financial situation.

Additionally, we reviewed consolidation and refinancing options, which offer ways to streamline multiple debts into single, manageable payments, potentially lowering interest rates and simplifying your financial obligations. By implementing these methods thoughtfully, you can ease financial stress and work towards a stronger financial future. As you continue to apply these principles, remember that maintaining a budget, building an emergency fund, and regularly monitoring your progress are essential steps in the journey to achieving financial stability and freedom.

Alex Knight

Chapter 7 : Income Streams and Side Hustles

Increasing one's income through multiple streams is a smart approach to achieving financial stability and freedom. This chapter delves into the diverse methods that individuals can utilize to create additional sources of income, thereby enhancing their overall financial portfolio. Emphasizing practical strategies, the aim is to provide actionable insights that can be implemented by working professionals and anyone keen on enhancing their financial literacy.

In this chapter, readers will explore various avenues for generating passive income, such as real estate investments, dividend-paying stocks, and digital products. The discussion will extend to innovative concepts like real estate crowdfunding and peer-to-peer lending, highlighting both their potential and associated risks. Furthermore, the chapter will examine popular side hustle opportunities, including freelancing, e-commerce, gig economy jobs, tutoring, and more. By evaluating these options, readers will gain a comprehensive understanding of how to diversify their income streams effectively, allowing them to make informed decisions tailored to their financial goals and personal circumstances.

Alex Knight

Passive Income Ideas

Passive income is a powerful way to diversify income streams, especially for those looking to achieve financial freedom. The concept revolves around earning money with minimal daily effort once the initial investment or setup is complete. This subpoint delves into various passive income avenues and their potential benefits for working professionals seeking to enhance their financial portfolios.

Real estate has long been considered a reliable source of passive income. Rental properties allow individuals to earn regular cash flow from tenants while potentially benefiting from property appreciation over time. Owning rental properties requires significant time and capital upfront, including property selection, financing, and tenant management. However, the rewards can be substantial, providing steady income and long-term financial growth.

An alternative to owning physical properties is real estate crowdfunding. This method allows investors to pool their resources to fund real estate projects, spreading the risk among many participants. Platforms like Fundrise and RealtyMogul have made it easier for individuals to invest in real estate without owning property directly. Investors receive returns through rental income and property appreciation, often with lower entry costs than traditional real estate investments. Crowdfunding offers diversification within real estate by allowing participation in different types of properties, such as residential, commercial, and industrial.

Another popular avenue for passive income is investing in dividend-paying stocks. Unlike growth stocks, which reinvest profits to fuel further company growth, dividend stocks distribute a portion of earnings to shareholders regularly. Companies in sectors like utilities, consumer goods, and telecommunications are known for paying consistent dividends. By building a diversified portfolio of dividend-paying stocks, investors can earn regular income while potentially benefiting from capital gains if stock prices increase. It's crucial to analyze a company's financial health and dividend history when selecting stocks, ensuring a sustainable income stream.

The online world also presents numerous opportunities for generating passive income. Creating digital products, such as e-books, courses, or software, can provide ongoing revenue with limited maintenance. For instance, an author who writes an e-book only needs to invest effort during the creation process; sales generate income without requiring further work. Similarly, online courses can attract students worldwide, offering repeated sales without additional labor post-launch.

Affiliate marketing is another lucrative option where individuals earn commissions by promoting other people's products. By incorporating affiliate links in blogs, social media, or YouTube channels, marketers can earn a percentage of sales generated through their referrals. Success in affiliate marketing hinges on choosing the right niche and cultivating a loyal audience that trusts product recommendations.

Dropshipping simplifies e-commerce by eliminating the need to manage inventory. Entrepreneurs create online stores, list products from suppliers, and forward customer orders to these suppliers, who ship directly to customers. Dropshipping reduces upfront costs and storage concerns, making it accessible to those with limited startup capital. However, careful research is essential to select reliable suppliers and high-demand products, ensuring customer satisfaction and sustained income.

Peer-to-peer lending (P2P) introduces another form of passive income through direct loans between individuals without traditional financial institutions. Platforms like LendingClub and Prosper connect lenders with borrowers, enabling lenders to earn interest on their investments. P2P lending allows for portfolio diversification by funding multiple loans, spreading risk across several borrowers. Understanding each borrower's creditworthiness and loan purpose helps mitigate potential defaults, although it's important to recognize that P2P lending carries inherent risks, such as borrower insolvency during economic downturns.

Evaluating risks and returns is critical when considering passive income sources. Real estate investments can be affected by market fluctuations, property damage, or tenant issues, emphasizing the importance of diligent property management. Diversifying real estate holdings and maintaining an emergency fund can mitigate some risks.

Dividend-paying stocks carry market and company-specific risks. Stock prices can fluctuate based on economic conditions, and companies may reduce or suspend dividends if facing financial difficulties. To counteract these risks, investing in well-established companies with strong track records and diversifying across different sectors is advisable.

Digital products require initial effort in development and marketing. Ensuring high-quality content and effective marketing strategies can lead to sustainable sales and passive income. Regular updates and customer engagement can boost product longevity and revenue.

Affiliate marketing's success depends on the marketer's ability to build trust with their audience. High competition and constantly changing algorithms of platforms like Google and Facebook can impact traffic and earnings. Researching profitable niches, producing valuable content, and staying updated with industry trends can enhance success.

Dropshipping faces challenges like supplier reliability and product quality. Building strong relationships with suppliers, maintaining clear communication, and providing excellent customer service are key to sustaining a dropshipping business. Monitoring market trends and adjusting product offerings can keep the business competitive.

In P2P lending, the primary risk is borrower default. Thoroughly assessing borrower profiles, diversifying loans across various credit grades, and staying informed about platform policies can help manage this risk. Considering the economic environment and personal risk tolerance is essential for successful P2P lending.

Side Hustle Opportunities

In today's dynamic economy, the appeal of side hustles has grown significantly. For working professionals and individuals eager to achieve financial freedom, supplementing income through diverse avenues can be both rewarding and practical. This section will delve into identifying various side hustle opportunities to help you boost your earnings and fast-track your financial objectives.

Freelancing stands as one of the most versatile side hustles available. Whether you excel in writing, graphic design, web development, or consulting, freelance work offers the opportunity to leverage your skills for additional income. Platforms such as Fiverr, Upwork, and Freelancer make it easier than ever to connect with clients seeking your expertise. Engaging in freelance work can provide flexible hours, allowing you to maintain your primary job while dedicating spare time to your side hustle. Additionally, freelancing enables you to build a portfolio and expand professional networks, which could lead to more lucrative contracts in the future.

Starting an e-commerce store is another viable option for those looking to diversify their income streams. With the advent of platforms like Shopify, Etsy, and Amazon, setting up an online store is more accessible than ever. You can sell handcrafted items, vintage finds, or even dropship products without holding inventory. The key to a successful e-commerce business lies in identifying a niche market, understanding customer needs, and effectively marketing your products. Social media marketing, search engine optimization (SEO), and influencer collaborations can significantly boost your store's visibility and sales. Moreover, running an e-commerce store allows you to scale your business at your own pace, making it a sustainable long-term side hustle.

Participating in the gig economy offers yet another path to supplemental income. Platforms such as Uber, TaskRabbit, and Upwork provide opportunities to earn money by performing various tasks, from driving passengers to assembling furniture or completing administrative work. Gig economy jobs often come with flexible schedules, enabling you to choose when and how much you want to work. This flexibility is particularly beneficial for those juggling multiple responsibilities. Furthermore, gig work can serve as a stepping stone to more substantial entrepreneurial ventures by helping you gain valuable experience, understand market demands, and build a client base.

Offering tutoring services or teaching classes is another excellent way to earn extra income. If you have expertise in specific subjects or possess unique skills, sharing your knowledge with others can be both fulfilling and profitable. Online platforms like VIPKid, Chegg Tutors, and Teachable facilitate connecting with students worldwide. Whether it's academic tutoring, language instruction, or teaching specialized skills like coding or photography, the demand for personal and professional development is high. Additionally, local community centers, schools, and libraries often seek instructors for various classes and workshops, providing further opportunities for in-person teaching.

To maximize the potential of these side hustles, here are some guidelines to consider:

1. **Assess Your Skills and Interests**: Identify what you are good at and passionate about. A side hustle that aligns with your strengths and interests is more likely to be enjoyable and sustainable.
2. **Time Management**: Balancing a side hustle with your primary job requires effective time management. Use tools like calendars, to-do lists, and productivity apps to schedule your tasks and avoid burnout.
3. **Market Research**: Conduct thorough research to understand the demand for your services or products. Analyze competitors, identify target audiences, and stay updated on market trends to make informed decisions.
4. **Financial Planning**: Set clear financial goals for your side hustle. Keep track of your income and expenses, and reinvest profits wisely to grow your venture.
5. **Quality Over Quantity**: Focus on delivering high-quality work or products. Building a reputation for excellence can lead to repeat business and positive word-of-mouth referrals.
6. **Continuous Learning**: Stay informed about industry developments and continuously upgrade your skills.

Taking online courses, attending workshops, and networking with peers can enhance your capabilities and keep you competitive.

Balancing Time and Effort

Balancing time and effort between primary income sources, side hustles, and personal life is a challenging yet vital skill for anyone looking to increase their income. One of the most critical aspects of achieving this balance is effective time management. Managing multiple income streams requires you to be organized and efficient with your time to avoid overwhelming yourself. Several tools and techniques can assist in this endeavor. For instance, using a daily planner or digital calendar can help you schedule tasks and prioritize activities. Time-blocking is another practical technique where you dedicate specific periods to different tasks, ensuring that you focus on one task at a time without distractions.

When juggling multiple income streams, it's crucial to establish boundaries to prevent burnout and maintain work-life balance. Setting clear limits on the amount of time you spend working on each income stream will help you avoid overworking and ensure you have time for rest and personal activities. For example, you might decide not to work on weekends or after a particular hour in the evening. Taking regular breaks throughout the day can also help keep stress levels down and improve productivity. Furthermore, communicating these boundaries to family and colleagues can help manage expectations and support your efforts to maintain a healthy work-life balance.

Monitoring the performance of your income streams is essential for evaluating their impact on your overall financial goals. Regularly reviewing and assessing how each income stream is performing will give you insights into which ones are more profitable and which ones may need more attention or adjustment. This could involve tracking your earnings, expenses, and time invested in each income stream. Analyzing this data will reveal patterns and trends that can inform your decisions about where to allocate your time and resources more effectively. Additionally, seeking feedback from clients or customers can provide valuable insights into areas for improvement and innovation.

Using metrics to assess the profitability of side hustles is another crucial aspect of managing multiple income streams. Different metrics can provide a comprehensive picture of how well your side hustles are doing. For instance, calculating the return on investment (ROI) can help you understand how much profit you are making relative to the time and money you invest. Other metrics, such as customer acquisition cost, lifetime value of a customer, and net profit margin, can offer deeper insights into various aspects of your side hustles' performance. By regularly analyzing these metrics, you can identify opportunities to increase efficiency, reduce costs, and boost profitability.

Time management tools like apps can play a significant role in organizing your multiple income streams. Apps such as Trello or Asana allow you to create task boards, set deadlines, and track progress, helping you stay on top of your tasks. Using automation tools for routine tasks can save valuable time. Automating repetitive tasks, such as invoicing or social media posts, frees up time that can be better spent on more productive activities. Learning and implementing these tools can streamline your workflow and make juggling multiple responsibilities more manageable.

To establish boundaries, creating a dedicated workspace can greatly enhance your productivity and focus. Working from a specific location can mentally prepare you for the tasks at hand and minimize distractions. Also, setting specific work hours and sticking to them can help you separate work from personal life. It's essential to communicate with your family or roommates about your work hours so they understand when you need uninterrupted time. Maintaining these boundaries consistently will help you develop a routine that supports both your professional and personal life.

In addition to setting physical and temporal boundaries, emotional boundaries are equally important. It's crucial to recognize when you're feeling overwhelmed or stressed and take proactive steps to address these feelings. Practicing self-care, whether through exercise, meditation, hobbies, or spending time with loved ones, can help you recharge and maintain a positive mindset. Being mindful of your mental health and taking care of your emotional well-being will enable you to approach your work with renewed energy and enthusiasm.

Regularly monitoring the performance of your income streams means setting aside time for weekly or monthly reviews. During these sessions, evaluate your earnings, compare them to your goals, and analyze any deviations. Tracking software like QuickBooks or Excel spreadsheets can help you organize and review financial data efficiently. By maintaining accurate records, you'll be able to make informed decisions about which income streams to scale up, modify, or potentially phase out if they're not meeting your expectations. Strategic adjustments based on data analysis will ensure your income streams contribute positively to your financial objectives.

Metrics that go beyond simple profit and loss calculations offer a more nuanced view of your side hustles' success. For instance, tracking engagement rates for online businesses or client retention rates for freelancing can provide insight into the long-term sustainability of your ventures. Understanding these metrics allows for targeted improvements. If certain products or services are underperforming, you can investigate underlying issues such as market demand, pricing strategies, or marketing effectiveness. A thorough analysis of these factors will equip you with the knowledge needed to optimize your side hustles and achieve consistent growth.

As you juggle multiple income streams, it's also important to remain adaptable. Market conditions, customer preferences, and economic factors are continuously changing, and being flexible in your approach will help you navigate these changes successfully. Continuously educating yourself and staying updated on industry trends will give you an edge in identifying new opportunities and adjusting your strategies accordingly. Embracing a mindset of continuous learning and adaptability ensures that you stay resilient and prepared to tackle challenges as they arise.

Another way to manage multiple income streams effectively is through networking and collaboration. Building a supportive network of like-minded individuals can provide valuable advice, share experiences, and inspire new ideas. Joining online forums, attending industry conferences, or participating in local business groups can expand your network and open doors to potential collaborations. Collaborating with others can also lead to shared projects, reducing individual workload and fostering mutual growth. Developing strong professional relationships will enhance your ability to balance and sustain multiple income streams over the long term.

Tax Considerations

Tax planning is crucial for anyone trying to diversify their income streams. Understanding the tax responsibilities associated with different types of income can help you make better financial decisions and avoid potential pitfalls. When you have multiple sources of income, such as passive income or side hustles, knowing how they are taxed is essential.

Firstly, it's important to determine the tax responsibilities associated with various income sources. Passive income, like rental income or earnings from investments, is often subject to different tax rules than earned income from a job or freelance work. For instance, rental income may come with deductible expenses, such as property maintenance and mortgage interest, reducing the taxable amount. However, it also requires careful record-keeping to ensure you're claiming all eligible deductions accurately.

Side hustles, on the other hand, generate earned income, which is typically subject to self-employment taxes. This means you'll not only pay federal and state income taxes but also Social Security and Medicare taxes. If your side hustle involves selling goods or services, you may also need to collect and remit sales tax, depending on your location and the nature of your business. It's essential to be aware of these obligations to avoid penalties and interest that can arise from underpayment.

Differentiating between earned income and investment income is another critical aspect of tax planning. Earned income includes wages, salaries, tips, and income from self-employment. This type of income is usually subject to higher tax rates compared to investment income. Investment income, such as dividends, interest, and capital gains, often enjoys favorable tax treatment. For example, long-term capital gains, which result from selling an asset held for over a year, are taxed at a lower rate than short-term gains or ordinary income.

Knowing the difference between these types of income allows you to plan more effectively. For instance, if a significant portion of your income comes from investments, you might benefit from holding onto assets longer to qualify for lower long-term capital gains rates. Additionally, certain investments like municipal bonds offer tax-exempt interest, providing tax savings opportunities.

Strategies for minimizing tax liabilities and maximizing tax savings are integral to efficient tax planning. One effective strategy is to maximize contributions to tax-advantaged accounts, such as 401(k) plans, IRAs, and Health Savings Accounts (HSAs).

Contributions to these accounts can reduce your taxable income, thereby lowering your overall tax liability. Another strategy is to take advantage of tax credits, such as the Earned Income Tax Credit (EITC), Child Tax Credit, and education credits. These credits directly reduce the amount of tax you owe and can result in significant savings.

Additionally, consider employing tax-loss harvesting if you have investment income. This strategy involves selling investments that have lost value to offset gains from other investments. By doing so, you can reduce your taxable capital gains. Similarly, timing your income and deductions can also be beneficial. For example, if you expect to be in a higher tax bracket next year, deferring income or accelerating deductions into the current year could lower your tax bill.

Maintaining accurate records of income and expenses is fundamental for tax reporting purposes. Good record-keeping practices not only help you stay organized but also ensure that you can substantiate any deductions or credits you claim. Keep receipts, invoices, and bank statements for all income and expenses related to your various income streams. Utilize financial software or apps to track your finances throughout the year, making tax time less stressful.

Keeping detailed records is especially important if you have a side hustle or earn passive income. For example, if you rent out a property, maintain documentation of all rental income received, as well as expenses like repairs, utilities, and property management fees. These records will be vital when preparing your tax return and can help you avoid underreporting income or missing out on deductible expenses.

Similarly, if you run a side hustle, keep track of all business-related expenses, such as supplies, advertising costs, and travel expenses. Proper documentation can support your claims for deductions and reduce your taxable income. In case of an audit, having thorough records can provide the necessary evidence to validate your tax positions.

Another aspect of good record-keeping is separating personal and business finances. Open a separate bank account and credit card for your side hustle or investment activities. This practice simplifies tracking income and expenses and reduces the risk of commingling funds, which can complicate tax reporting and lead to errors.

Evaluating Risks and Returns

In today's fast-paced financial landscape, diversifying your income streams can offer significant potential gains, but it also presents a myriad of risks. One of the most popular options for passive income is real estate. Buying property to rent out can be a steady source of monthly revenue. For instance, owning an apartment in a bustling urban area can generate consistent rental income. However, the benefits go beyond just rent; property values tend to appreciate over time, which could mean substantial profits if you decide to sell in the future. Moreover, real estate often serves as a hedge against inflation since property values and rental rates usually rise with inflation.

However, investing in real estate isn't without its challenges. Property maintenance, dealing with tenants, and fluctuating market conditions can be significant obstacles. It's crucial to perform thorough research and perhaps consult a real estate expert before making any investments. Also, consider the location carefully; areas with higher job growth and amenities often attract more tenants and higher rents. Understanding these nuances can make a world of difference in maximizing returns while mitigating risks.

Switching gears, another avenue to explore is dividend stock investments. Dividend-paying stocks can provide regular income in the form of dividends, along with the potential for capital appreciation. Companies that consistently pay dividends are typically well-established and financially stable. This can make dividend stocks an attractive option for those looking for a relatively low-risk investment. For example, many renowned companies like Coca-Cola or Johnson & Johnson have been paying consistent dividends over decades, offering reliability to investors.

Nevertheless, dividend stocks come with their own set of risks. Market volatility can affect the stock price, and there's always the possibility that a company might reduce or eliminate its dividend payments due to financial difficulties. It's essential to analyze the company's dividend payout ratio, history, and overall financial health before investing. Diversification is key; spreading investments across multiple sectors can help mitigate risks associated with economic downturns in specific industries.

When it comes to online business models, the plethora of choices can be overwhelming. Selecting the right model depends on various factors, including your skillset, interests, and available time. E-commerce, blogging, and affiliate marketing are some common options. E-commerce ventures require a keen understanding of market demand, product sourcing, and customer service. Platforms like Shopify make it easier for beginners to set up an online store, but success still requires rigorous planning and execution.

Blogging and affiliate marketing, on the other hand, can be less demanding in terms of initial capital. A blog can be monetized through advertisements, sponsored posts, or affiliate links. The primary challenge here is generating enough traffic to make these monetization methods viable. Consistently creating high-quality content that resonates with your target audience is crucial for success in this sphere. Analyze successful blogs in your niche to understand what works and implement similar strategies in your platform.

Peer-to-peer (P2P) lending has emerged as another intriguing option for those seeking to diversify their portfolios. P2P lending allows you to loan money directly to individuals or small businesses through online platforms, such as LendingClub or Prosper. These platforms connect lenders with borrowers and handle loan servicing, making it a relatively hands-off investment once you've chosen where to allocate your funds. The returns can be quite attractive compared to traditional savings accounts or bonds, but they come with elevated risks.

To mitigate these risks, diversification within your P2P lending portfolio is critical. Spreading your investment across numerous loans rather than committing a large sum to a single borrower can help cushion the blow if one or more loans default. Additionally, it's vital to scrutinize the creditworthiness of borrowers. Most P2P platforms provide ratings based on credit scores, income levels, and other factors, helping you make more informed decisions. Always start small and gradually increase your investments as you become more comfortable with the process and platform.

While each of these income streams offers unique advantages and drawbacks, careful planning, research, and diversification can enhance your chances of financial success. The objective is not solely to maximize returns but to create a balanced portfolio that aligns with your risk tolerance and financial goals. Investing in real estate may offer stable cash flow and long-term appreciation, but it requires substantial initial capital and ongoing management. Dividend stocks can provide reliable income, though they are subject to market fluctuations. Choosing the right online business model hinges on your personal strengths and market conditions, while peer-to-peer lending demands prudent diversification to manage risk effectively.

Final Thoughts

In this chapter, we've explored various methods for enhancing income through multiple streams, focusing on passive income and side hustle opportunities. From real estate investments to online business ventures, each avenue offers unique benefits and challenges. Understanding the dynamics of these income sources, such as rental properties, dividend-paying stocks, and e-commerce, enables you to make informed decisions tailored to your financial goals. Assessing the risks and returns associated with each option is essential in developing a diversified and resilient financial portfolio.

Balancing time and effort across different income streams requires effective time management and clear boundaries to maintain work-life harmony. Utilizing tools like digital calendars and task management apps can streamline tasks and prevent burnout. Setting specific work hours and creating dedicated workspaces support productivity and focus. Regularly reviewing the performance of your income streams helps in adjusting strategies and optimizing profitability. By adopting these practices, you can navigate the complexities of managing multiple income sources while achieving financial growth and stability.

Chapter 8 : Planning for Retirement

Planning for retirement involves more than just saving money; it requires a comprehensive understanding of your future financial needs and the strategies available to meet them. It's important to consider various aspects such as estimating expenses, accounting for inflation, and planning for healthcare costs. Without a well-thought-out plan, you risk facing financial challenges during your retirement years that could have been mitigated with proper preparation.

In this chapter, we will explore key strategies to ensure your financial security in retirement. We will guide you through the process of accurately estimating your future expenses based on your current lifestyle and how to adjust these estimations to account for inflation. Additionally, the chapter will cover important considerations like healthcare costs, the impact of longevity, and the potential benefits of consulting financial experts. By understanding these elements, you will be better equipped to create a tailored retirement plan that supports your desired lifestyle while safeguarding your financial future.

Understanding Retirement Needs

Understanding your retirement financial needs is crucial for ensuring a comfortable and financially secure future. By accurately estimating your expenses, considering your desired lifestyle, and consulting financial experts, you can create a tailored plan that aligns with your retirement goals.

Estimating your retirement expenses starts with knowing your current living costs. This means tracking your monthly and annual spending on essentials like housing, food, transportation, and utilities. Additionally, it's important to consider discretionary expenses such as travel, hobbies, and dining out, which will likely continue into retirement. Once you have a clear picture of your current expenses, you can begin to estimate future needs by factoring in inflation.

Inflation affects the purchasing power of money over time, meaning the cost of goods and services will increase as you age. For instance, if the average annual inflation rate is 3%, something that costs $1,000 today will cost approximately $1,344 in ten years. Therefore, it's essential to project your expenses under different inflation scenarios to ensure that your savings keep pace with rising costs. Healthcare costs also play a significant role in retirement planning. As you grow older, healthcare expenses generally increase due to greater need for medical care and long-term services. According to some estimates, an average retired couple might need upwards of $300,000 to cover healthcare expenses during retirement. To avoid underestimating these costs, consider including a separate healthcare inflation rate in your projections.

Knowing your current expenses is crucial for calculating your future financial needs. One effective way to estimate these is by using detailed budgeting tools or calculators that help map out anticipated costs. These tools enable you to input various factors like your expected retirement age, current savings, anticipated Social Security benefits, and other income sources. They also allow for adjustments, providing you with multiple scenarios to see how changes in spending or saving patterns can affect your retirement outlook.

Your retirement vision plays an important role in defining your financial needs. Different lifestyles require different levels of financial support, so it's important to adapt your savings plan accordingly. For instance, if you envision a quiet life in a small town, your expenses might be relatively low. Conversely, if you plan to spend your retirement traveling extensively or indulging in expensive hobbies, you'll need a significantly larger nest egg. Creating a realistic budget for your envisioned lifestyle involves listing all potential expenses and categorizing them into essential and discretionary costs. Essential costs include food, housing, and healthcare, while discretionary costs encompass entertainment, travel, and other personal interests. This process helps highlight areas where you could adjust your spending to achieve your desired lifestyle without compromising financial security.

It's also useful to consider the longevity factor when planning for different lifestyles. Since no one can predict exactly how long they'll live, planning up to age 95 or beyond ensures that your funds last throughout your lifetime. Additionally, consider whether you plan to continue working part-time during retirement or fully retire from the workforce. Part-time work can supplement your income and reduce the strain on your retirement savings. While dreaming of your ideal retirement, it's wise to incorporate flexibility into your plans. Life is unpredictable, and your priorities may change over time. The ability to adapt your financial strategy ensures you're prepared for unforeseen circumstances or shifts in your retirement goals.

Consulting financial experts can provide customized guidance and valuable insights into your retirement needs. Financial advisors use various tools and calculators to help you create accurate projections based on your individual circumstances. These professionals analyze your current financial situation, taking into account factors such as income, expenses, investment returns, and retirement age. They then offer tailored advice on optimizing your savings and investments to meet your retirement objectives. Tools like the Complete Retirement Planner, NewRetirement Calculator, and Playing With Fire Retirement Calculator are designed to give comprehensive financial forecasts. For example, the Complete Retirement Planner includes information on inflation, tax laws, Medicare costs, and Social Security benefits, helping you evaluate the best time to start withdrawing from retirement accounts (Hartman et al., 2023).

Additionally, advanced retirement planning software such as WealthTrace and Titan offers in-depth analyses of your financial and retirement situation. These tools allow you to link your accounts, automatically update balances, and run different scenarios to see how changes in your savings strategy can impact your retirement outcomes. Titan's calculator, for instance, projects your retirement needs based on historical growth rates, with options to adjust for more aggressive or conservative investment strategies. It also assumes salary increases and inflation rates for more accurate forecasting *(Best Retirement Calculator (2019) - See How Much You'll Need | SmartAsset.com, 2019).*

Working with a financial advisor can also help you navigate complex topics such as tax implications, optimal asset allocation, and risk management. Advisors provide recommendations on balancing your portfolio to align with your risk tolerance and investment goals. They can also guide you through tax-efficient withdrawal strategies, ensuring you make the most of your retirement savings while minimizing tax liabilities. Finding the right fit among digital tools and professional advice depends on how detailed you want your retirement plan to be. Some tools offer overviews, while others walk you through every step, providing a high level of detail.

Types of Retirement Accounts

When planning for retirement, understanding the various account options can make a significant difference in achieving financial security. Let's explore some key retirement accounts starting with 401(k) plans and IRAs.

401(k) Plans and IRAs

A 401(k) is an employer-sponsored retirement savings plan that allows employees to save and invest a portion of their paycheck before taxes are taken out. Assessing eligibility typically involves being employed by a company that offers this type of plan. Contribution limits for a 401(k) are determined annually by the IRS. As of 2020, employees can contribute up to $19,500, with an additional catch-up contribution of $6,500 for those aged 50 and older *(Kagan, 2022)*.

One of the main benefits of a 401(k) is the potential for employer matching. Many employers offer to match employee contributions up to a certain percentage of salary, which essentially provides free money towards your retirement fund. This feature makes 401(k) plans highly attractive. However, it's crucial to understand the terms of vesting schedules, as some employer contributions might require you to stay with the company for a number of years before fully owning these funds.

Next, we have Individual Retirement Accounts (IRAs), which come in several types, the most common being Traditional IRAs and Roth IRAs. With a Traditional IRA, contributions may be tax-deductible depending on your income and other factors, and the earnings grow tax-deferred until withdrawn. The annual contribution limit for IRAs in 2020 is $6,000, with a $1,000 catch-up contribution for those aged 50 and over (Inc et al., n.d.).

Understanding withdrawal rules is essential. For both 401(k)s and Traditional IRAs, early withdrawals before age 59½ typically incur a 10% penalty on top of ordinary income taxes, though there are exceptions such as first-time home purchases or higher education expenses. Required minimum distributions (RMDs) must begin at age 72, ensuring the government eventually collects its tax revenue from these accounts.

Roth vs. Traditional IRAs

Deciding between Roth and Traditional IRAs hinges on understanding their tax implications. Contributions to a Traditional IRA are often deductible, reducing your taxable income in the year you contribute. Conversely, Roth IRAs are funded with after-tax dollars, meaning contributions are not deductible. However, qualified withdrawals from Roth IRAs are entirely tax-free, which can be advantageous if you anticipate being in a higher tax bracket in retirement.

For many, the choice between the two depends on current versus future tax expectations. If you expect to be in a higher tax bracket when you retire, a Roth IRA could be more beneficial. On the other hand, if you are currently in a high tax bracket but expect it to be lower in retirement, a Traditional IRA might save you money overall.

Another consideration is flexibility. Unlike Traditional IRAs, Roth IRAs do not require RMDs during the owner's lifetime, allowing the account to grow tax-free for longer. This characteristic makes Roth IRAs especially appealing for those who plan to leave money to heirs.

Other Retirement Vehicles

Beyond 401(k)s and IRAs, there are several other retirement vehicles tailored for specific needs and employment scenarios. Simplified Employee Pension (SEP) IRAs are designed for self-employed individuals and small business owners. They allow much higher contribution limits than Traditional IRAs, up to 25% of compensation or $57,000 annually in 2020 (Kagan, 2022). SEP IRAs are easy to set up and maintain, making them a popular choice among freelancers and sole proprietors.

SIMPLE IRAs (Savings Incentive Match Plan for Employees) serve small businesses with fewer than 100 employees. Like a 401(k), employers are required to either match employee contributions or make nonelective contributions. SIMPLE IRAs have lower contribution limits compared to SEP IRAs but still offer an attractive way to save, with an annual limit of $13,500 plus a $3,000 catch-up contribution for individuals aged 50 or older.

For self-employed individuals, solo 401(k) plans combine the benefits of a standard 401(k) and a profit-sharing plan. Solo 401(k)s permit high contribution limits, up to $57,000 annually (or $63,500 including catch-up contributions). These plans offer both pre-tax (traditional) and post-tax (Roth) options within the same account, providing excellent flexibility.

Choosing the right retirement vehicle involves assessing your specific situation. Freelancers and independent contractors might prefer SEP IRAs for their ease and high contribution limits, while small business employees might benefit more from SIMPLE IRAs due to mandatory employer contributions. Meanwhile, solo 401(k)s cater well to self-employed individuals looking for higher contribution thresholds and flexible investment options.

To make informed decisions, it's advisable to periodically review your retirement plans and consider consulting financial advisors who can provide personalized guidance. Regularly updating your knowledge about contribution limits, tax benefits, and new regulations will also help ensure you're optimizing your retirement strategy effectively.

Investment Strategies for Retirement

Investing for retirement can be complex, but understanding some core principles of effective investment strategies can pave the way for a financially secure retirement. This section aims to provide practical guidance on how to effectively invest for your retirement goals by focusing on three key areas: asset allocation, risk management, and income generation.

Asset Allocation

Asset allocation is the process of spreading investments across various asset classes such as stocks, bonds, and other securities to balance risk and reward. The primary goal of asset allocation is to optimize your portfolio's performance while minimizing potential risks.

One fundamental approach to asset allocation is to diversify your investments. Diversification helps mitigate risk by ensuring that poor performance in one area can potentially be offset by better performance in another. For example, investing in a mix of stocks and bonds can reduce risk because these assets typically perform differently under the same market conditions. Stocks might offer higher returns but come with greater volatility, whereas bonds generally provide more stable but lower returns.

A well-rounded portfolio tailored to your risk tolerance and time horizon is essential. Younger investors with longer time horizons might choose to allocate a larger portion of their portfolio to stocks since they have more time to recover from market downturns. Conversely, older investors nearing retirement might shift towards bonds and other fixed-income securities to preserve capital and minimize volatility. The seminal work by Markowitz on modern portfolio theory supports this approach, highlighting the benefits of combining non-correlated assets to achieve an optimal balance between risk and return *(Portfolio Theory, Life-Cycle Investing, and Retirement Income, 2007)*.

Risk Management

Effective risk management is crucial to protect your retirement savings from market volatility. One strategy involves regular rebalancing of your portfolio. Rebalancing is the process of realigning the weightings of your portfolio's asset classes back to your original target allocations. This is necessary because over time, some investments may grow faster than others, shifting your portfolio's risk profile. By rebalancing, you ensure that you maintain your desired level of risk.

Another aspect of risk management is assessing your risk tolerance, which is your ability and willingness to endure market fluctuations. Risk tolerance varies from person to person and is influenced by factors such as age, financial goals, and individual comfort levels with risk. A periodic review of your risk tolerance helps you make informed decisions about adjusting your investment strategy.

Utilizing retirement calculators and tools can help project future needs accurately and determine whether your current investment strategy aligns with your long-term goals. These tools consider variables such as expected rate of return, inflation, and life expectancy to provide a clearer picture of your retirement readiness. Employing these tools allows you to make data-driven decisions and adjust your investment plan as needed to stay on track.

Income Generation

Generating sustainable income during retirement is a critical aspect of retirement planning. Several strategies and financial products can help ensure a steady stream of income.

Dividends from stock investments can provide a reliable income source. Dividends are payments made by companies to shareholders out of their profits. Choosing dividend-paying stocks, especially those with a history of consistent payouts, can supplement your retirement income. However, it's important to research and select companies with strong financial health to mitigate the risk of dividend cuts.

Annuities are another option to consider for generating retirement income. An annuity is a financial product that provides regular payments in exchange for a lump-sum investment. There are various types of annuities, including immediate and deferred annuities. Immediate annuities start paying out almost immediately after the initial investment, making them suitable for those who need income right away. Deferred annuities, on the other hand, begin payouts at a later date, allowing your investment to grow tax-deferred until you start receiving payments. Annuities can offer guaranteed income for life, providing peace of mind that you won't outlive your assets.

Withdrawal strategies also play a significant role in managing retirement income. The commonly known 4% rule suggests withdrawing 4% of your retirement savings in the first year of retirement and adjusting that amount annually for inflation. This rule aims to provide a steady income stream while preserving the principal over a long retirement period. However, it's crucial to customize your withdrawal strategy based on your unique financial situation, life expectancy, and market conditions. More flexible approaches, such as dynamic withdrawal strategies, allow for adjustments in spending based on portfolio performance, offering greater adaptability to changing circumstances.

The Role of Social Security

Understanding the impact and considerations of Social Security is crucial for a comprehensive retirement plan. For many, Social Security represents a significant portion of their retirement income, so grasping its intricacies can help optimize benefits and ensure financial security in later years.

Social Security Basics
Social Security benefits are primarily calculated based on your earnings throughout your working life. The Social Security Administration (SSA) uses your highest 35 years of earnings to compute your average indexed monthly earnings (AIME). The AIME is then used to determine your primary insurance amount (PIA), which is the benefit you will receive at full retirement age (FRA).

The concept of FRA is fundamental. It is the age at which you're entitled to receive 100% of your PIA. For those born between 1943 and 1954, the FRA is 66. For those born in 1960 or later, it is 67. It's important to note that while you can start claiming benefits as early as age 62, doing so will reduce your monthly benefit amount. Conversely, delaying benefits past your FRA increases your benefit by approximately 8% per year until age 70. This decision requires careful consideration of your financial needs, health status, and life expectancy.

Early versus delayed benefits present crucial trade-offs. Claiming early may be beneficial if you need immediate income or have health concerns that could limit your lifespan. However, delaying benefits can increase the total amount you'll receive over your lifetime, making it a powerful tool for maximizing retirement income.

Optimization Strategies
To make the most of your Social Security benefits, consider

several optimization strategies. One effective approach is exploring spousal benefits. If you are married, you can claim benefits based on your own earnings record or up to 50% of your spouse's PIA, whichever is higher. This strategy is advantageous if one spouse has significantly lower lifetime earnings. Additionally, if you delay your own benefits beyond FRA, your spouse can still begin collecting spousal benefits, providing a flexible income stream.

Survivor benefits also play a critical role in retirement planning. If your spouse passes away, you can claim either your own benefit or up to 100% of your deceased spouse's benefit, whichever is higher. This ensures that surviving spouses can maintain an adequate income level. In cases of remarriage, timing is key; marrying before age 60 disqualifies you from receiving survivor benefits based on your former spouse's record, while remarrying after age 60 does not.

Claiming strategies such as the "file and suspend" method, though largely phased out, previously allowed one spouse to file for benefits and then immediately suspend them to enable the other spouse to claim spousal benefits. While this loophole has been closed, understanding historical and current rules helps ensure you don't miss opportunities for optimal benefit claims.

Long-Term Outlook
Planning for the long-term outlook of Social Security involves anticipating potential changes and incorporating them into a broader retirement strategy. Social Security faces funding challenges, with projections indicating that the trust funds may

face shortfalls in the coming decades. While benefits are unlikely to disappear, potential reforms could include reduced benefits or increased eligibility ages.

Incorporating potential changes into your retirement plan ensures you're prepared for any adjustments. This involves diversifying your sources of retirement income, such as pensions, savings, and investments, to mitigate reliance on Social Security alone. By adopting a multi-faceted approach, you can protect yourself against expected future reforms.

Comprehensive retirement income strategy entails regular monitoring and adjusting of your plans. Regularly review your Social Security statements to verify your earnings records and predicted benefits. Correct any discrepancies promptly, as inaccuracies could affect your future benefits. Use online calculators and tools provided by the SSA to estimate the impact of different claiming ages and evaluate how various scenarios align with your financial goals.

Another aspect of the long-term outlook includes accounting for inflation. Social Security benefits are adjusted annually through cost-of-living adjustments (COLAs) to preserve purchasing power, but these adjustments may not always keep pace with actual increases in living costs. Understanding COLAs helps you anticipate and plan for inflationary pressures affecting your overall retirement budget.

Seeking professional advice can further enhance your retirement planning efforts. Financial advisors specializing in Social Security can offer tailored guidance based on your unique circumstances, helping you navigate complex decisions and legislation. They can provide insights into efficient claiming strategies, tax implications, and how best to integrate Social Security with other retirement assets.

It's also vital to stay informed about legislative changes impacting Social Security. Proactive engagement in ongoing education about retirement planning equips you with the knowledge needed to adapt to policy shifts and economic conditions, ensuring your retirement plan remains robust and responsive.

Long-term Care Planning

Preparing for health-related and long-term care needs during retirement is crucial for ensuring a financially stable and stress-free post-retirement life. As you plan for retirement, addressing potential health care costs, considering long-term care insurance, and setting up advanced directives are essential steps to take.

Health Care Costs: As you age, medical expenses tend to increase significantly. It is important to estimate these costs and devise a plan to cover them. According to Fidelity, a single person aged 65 in 2023 might need about $157,500 saved after tax to cover health care expenses in retirement, while an average couple might need around $315,000 *(Lake, 2023)*. These figures highlight the importance of planning ahead. One effective approach is to make the most out of Health Savings Accounts (HSAs). If your employer offers an HSA-eligible health plan, consider enrolling and contributing to it. HSAs allow you to save pre-tax dollars that can grow and be withdrawn tax-free for qualified medical expenses, providing a tax-efficient way to prepare for future health care costs *(How to Plan for Rising Health Care Costs | Fidelity, 2019)*.

Long-Term Care Insurance: Another critical aspect of preparing for retirement is evaluating your options for long-term care insurance. Long-term care refers to the assistance needed when one can no longer perform basic daily activities independently. This type of care can be expensive, and relying solely on personal savings or government programs like Medicaid may not suffice. By investing in long-term care insurance, you can mitigate the financial risk associated with requiring assisted living or nursing home care. Start by exploring different policies, comparing coverage options, premiums, and benefits. Understanding the specific terms and conditions of each policy will help you select the most appropriate plan for your needs. Additionally, some policies offer inflation protection, which can be beneficial in keeping up with rising health care costs over time (Administration for Community Living).

Advanced Directives: Preparing for potential medical situations where you might be unable to communicate your wishes is just as important. Advanced directives are legal documents that outline your preferences for medical care if you become incapacitated. There are primarily two types of advanced directives: a living will and a durable power of attorney for health care. A living will provides instructions on the types of medical treatment you would or would not want under certain circumstances. On the other hand, a durable power of attorney for health care designates a trusted person to make medical decisions on your behalf. Having these documents in place ensures that your medical care aligns with your values and desires, alleviating the burden on your loved ones during difficult times.

Final Insights

Ensuring a financially secure retirement is a multifaceted process that requires careful planning and informed decisions. Throughout this chapter, we have explored essential strategies including understanding your retirement needs, accurately estimating future expenses, and considering different lifestyle choices. We emphasized the importance of factoring in inflation and healthcare costs, as well as the benefits of using budgeting tools and consulting financial experts to create tailored plans.

By integrating detailed projections and flexible approaches, you can better prepare for the uncertainties of retirement. Embracing diverse investment strategies, leveraging various retirement accounts, and seeking professional advice are key steps toward achieving long-term financial stability. As you navigate your retirement journey, remember to periodically review and adjust your plans to align with changing circumstances and goals.

Chapter 9: Insurance and Risk Management

Insurance plays a vital role in managing financial risks and providing security against unforeseen events. It is a tool that helps individuals protect their health, property, income, and dependents from potential financial hardships. By understanding the various types of insurance available, such as health, auto, home, and life insurance, individuals can make informed decisions to safeguard their assets and ensure financial stability. This chapter delves into the importance of insurance and guides readers on how to select the right types to effectively manage different risks.

In this chapter, readers will explore the essential aspects of four main types of insurance: health, auto, home, and life insurance. Each section will cover the specific coverage options available within these categories, highlighting their benefits and significance. Additionally, the chapter will provide insights into evaluating personal circumstances to determine suitable insurance coverage, considering factors like age, health condition, and financial obligations. With practical examples and scenarios, readers will gain a clear understanding of how to assess their unique insurance needs and make well-informed choices to protect themselves and their loved ones.

Types of Insurance (Health, Auto, Home, Life)

Understanding the various types of insurance available is crucial for effectively managing potential risks. Let's explore different health insurance coverage options and their significance in managing unexpected medical expenses. Health insurance offers vital financial protection by covering a portion of healthcare costs, reducing the financial burden during medical emergencies. Common types of health insurance include employer-sponsored plans, individual health policies, and government programs like Medicare and Medicaid.

Employer-sponsored health insurance typically provides comprehensive coverage, including doctor visits, hospital stays, prescription drugs, and preventive care. Individual health policies, on the other hand, offer flexibility for those without access to employer plans, allowing them to customize coverage based on personal needs and budget. Government programs such as Medicare and Medicaid serve specific populations, like seniors and low-income individuals, ensuring they receive necessary medical care without incurring overwhelming expenses.

Understanding the importance of health insurance for unexpected medical expenses is critical. Unforeseen medical issues can arise at any time, leading to significant financial strain. With health insurance, individuals can access essential medical services without worrying about the high costs associated with treatments, surgeries, or prolonged hospital stays. This financial safety net ensures that medical emergencies do not derail one's personal finances and allows for timely and appropriate medical intervention.

Auto insurance is another essential type of coverage that safeguards against risks related to vehicle ownership and operation. Every driver must understand the legal requirements for auto insurance, which vary by state but generally include liability coverage for bodily injury and property damage. Liability coverage protects individuals from financial responsibility if they are at fault in an accident, covering the medical expenses and property repairs for the other party involved.

In addition to mandatory liability coverage, drivers can opt for additional coverage options that enhance their protection. Uninsured/underinsured motorist coverage provides financial assistance if an accident involves a driver who lacks adequate insurance. Comprehensive coverage protects against non-collision-related damages, such as theft, vandalism, or natural disasters. Collision coverage pays for repair or replacement costs if the insured's vehicle is damaged in an accident, regardless of fault. Medical payments coverage and personal injury protection (PIP) cover medical expenses for the policyholder and passengers, regardless of fault.

Several factors influence auto insurance premiums, including the driver's age, gender, driving history, location, and type of vehicle.

Insurance companies use these factors to assess risk and determine premium rates. For instance, young male drivers often face higher premiums due to statistically higher accident rates compared to middle-aged married men with extensive driving experience.

Home insurance is integral to protecting one's property and belongings. Different types of coverage provided by home insurance policies cater to various risks homeowners might face. Standard home insurance policies generally include dwelling coverage, personal property coverage, liability protection, and additional living expenses coverage.

Dwelling coverage insures the physical structure of the home against perils such as fire, windstorms, and hail. Personal property coverage protects belongings inside the home, such as furniture, electronics, and clothing. Liability protection covers legal expenses and damages if someone is injured on the property or if the homeowner accidentally causes damage to someone else's property. Additional living expenses coverage helps pay for temporary housing and other costs if the home is uninhabitable due to covered damages.

Choosing the right home insurance policy requires evaluating individual needs and circumstances. Homeowners should assess the value of their property and belongings to ensure adequate coverage. It's also important to consider the location and potential risks specific to the area, such as flood or earthquake hazards, which may require additional coverage options. Comparing quotes from multiple insurers and reviewing policy terms carefully can help homeowners find the best coverage at a reasonable price.

Life insurance is another critical component of a comprehensive risk management strategy. There are various life insurance policies, each serving different purposes and offering unique benefits. Term life insurance provides coverage for a specified period, usually 10, 20, or 30 years, and pays a death benefit if the policyholder passes away during the term. It is often chosen for its affordability and straightforward nature.

Whole life insurance, on the other hand, offers lifelong coverage and includes a cash value component that grows over time. Policyholders can borrow against the cash value or use it as collateral for loans. Universal life insurance combines the features of term and whole life insurance, providing flexible premiums and death benefits along with a cash value component that earns interest.

Assessing personal circumstances is essential when determining suitable life insurance coverage. Individuals should consider factors such as age, health condition, income level, family obligations, and long-term financial goals. For example, a young parent with dependent children might prioritize securing sufficient coverage to replace lost income and cover future expenses like education and mortgage payments. In contrast, older individuals nearing retirement might focus on final expense planning and leaving a legacy for heirs.

Alex Knight

Assessing Your Insurance Needs

Understanding one's unique insurance needs is a critical step in managing financial risks effectively. Each individual's circumstances, whether they pertain to personal health, property, or income, vary significantly, necessitating a personalized approach to determining appropriate insurance coverage.

Conducting a Personalized Risk Assessment

The first step in evaluating insurance requirements is conducting a personalized risk assessment. This process involves identifying potential risks and the areas of one's life that require protection. Start by considering all aspects of your daily life, including your health, home, vehicle, income, and any dependents you may have. Assessing these areas helps pinpoint specific risks that could lead to significant financial loss if not adequately insured.

For example, homeowners must consider risks such as natural disasters, theft, or damage to property. Those who own vehicles need to evaluate the potential costs associated with accidents, theft, and repairs. Moreover, individuals should not overlook health-related risks, which can lead to substantial medical expenses without proper coverage. By systematically analyzing each aspect of your life, you can better understand where insurance is necessary for safeguarding against unforeseen events.

Evaluating Financial Risks and Determining Protection Levels

Once the risk assessment is complete, the next step is to evaluate financial risks and determine the level of protection needed for different assets. This evaluation involves understanding the financial impact of various risks and deciding on the extent of coverage required to mitigate those impacts.

Take into account your current financial situation, including your income, savings, and outstanding debts. For instance, if you are the primary breadwinner, it's crucial to have sufficient life insurance to replace your income in case of an untimely death. This ensures that your family remains financially stable. According to Source 1, life insurance policies should ideally cover at least ten times your annual salary to replace lost income effectively (Beattie, 2023). Similarly, when considering health insurance, evaluate potential medical costs and ensure your policy covers significant health risks without inducing financial strain. It's also essential to consider deductibles and co-pays, which can affect out-of-pocket expenses.

Estimating Asset Values and Calculating Adequate Coverage

Estimating the value of your assets and calculating adequate coverage is another critical component of evaluating insurance requirements. Accurately valuation enables you to determine how much insurance you need to protect your possessions adequately. Begin by listing all tangible and intangible assets, such as your home, car, valuable personal items, and even future earning potential.

For property insurance, this means assessing the cost to repair or replace your home in the event of damage. Real estate appraisals and market comparisons can help in estimating these values accurately. Similarly, for auto insurance, consider the replacement cost of your vehicle and the financial implications of potential liabilities arising from accidents. In this context, using tools like online insurance estimators can provide a baseline for the coverage amount required to secure your assets effectively.

Life insurance computations can be more complex as they need to factor in future earnings, inflation, and potential financial obligations, such as children's education or spouse's retirement needs. According to Source 2, multiple factors influence the calculation of life insurance needs, including life stage, family status, income level, and liabilities *(3 Factors to Help Determine How Much Life Insurance You Need | F&G, n.d.)*. These elements collectively help in arriving at a comprehensive coverage figure.

Factoring in Potential Liabilities

A thorough evaluation of insurance needs must also include factoring in potential liabilities to ensure comprehensive protection. Liabilities represent financial burdens that could arise due to unforeseen events. They include outstanding debts like mortgages, credit card balances, car loans, and other personal loans. If these debts are not addressed through appropriate insurance coverage, they could become a significant financial burden for your dependents.

When calculating the necessary coverage, combine the total of all outstanding debts with additional funds to cover any accruing interest or fees. For example, if you have a $200,000 mortgage and a $10,000 car loan, your life insurance policy should at least cover these amounts, preferably with an added buffer to handle extra charges (Beattie, 2023). This ensures that in the event of your untimely demise, your dependents will not be left with overwhelming debt.

Additionally, consider potential legal liabilities. If you are a business owner or in a profession where lawsuits are common, obtaining liability insurance becomes paramount. This type of insurance protects against lawsuits for injuries or damages that occur on your property or as a result of your professional activities. Liability insurance keeps you safeguarded against potentially crippling legal expenses and judgments.

Practical Examples and Scenarios

To illustrate, let's consider a working professional who owns a home, has two cars, and supports a family. The individual's risk assessment reveals potential risks like property damage, vehicle accidents, health issues, and income loss. Financially, they carry a mortgage, car loans, and wish to ensure their children's college tuition is covered.

After evaluating their financial risks, they decide to obtain homeowner's insurance covering the full replacement cost of their house, comprehensive auto insurance for both vehicles, a robust health insurance plan with reasonable deductibles, and life insurance equal to ten times their annual salary. Additionally, they include riders to cover critical illnesses and disability, ensuring comprehensive protection across different scenarios.

The individual estimates the value of their home using recent market data and assessments, calculates potential automobile repair and replacement costs, and considers the average annual increase in healthcare expenses. Their life insurance coverage calculation includes their current debts, adding some buffer to account for future educational expenses for their children.

By incorporating potential liabilities, the scenario further solidifies the adequacy of their insurance coverage. Ensuring their life insurance covers all outstanding debts and future financial obligations protects their family from financial hardships during unpredictable, adverse situations.

Conclusion

Comparison Shopping for Insurance

When it comes to making informed decisions about insurance, the first step is exploring different insurance companies. This involves checking their reputation and financial stability. A reputable company with a solid financial background is critical because it ensures that the company can cover claims when necessary. Tools like AM Best's financial strength ratings and customer reviews from sources such as Better Business Bureau (BBB) or online forums can provide valuable insights into an insurer's reliability.

Comparing pricing and coverage options from multiple insurers is another essential step. Prices can vary significantly between companies for the same type of coverage. Thus, obtaining quotes from various providers and comparing them is necessary. This process allows you to weigh the cost against the benefits of each policy. For instance, while one provider might offer lower premiums, another might include more comprehensive coverage at a slightly higher price. Consider using comparison websites or contacting insurance agents to gather these quotes quickly and efficiently.

Understanding complex insurance terms and conditions is a crucial aspect of selecting the right policy. Insurance documents often contain jargon that can be confusing. Terms like "premium," "deductible," and "policy limit" are just a few examples. Delving into these terms helps in grasping what each policy entails and how it will function in various scenarios. For example, a deductible is the amount you pay out-of-pocket before the insurance company starts covering a claim. Knowing this can help you choose a policy that balances affordability with adequate protection.

Policy limits are another critical factor to understand. These limits dictate the maximum amount an insurer will pay for a covered loss. If your losses exceed these limits, you'll need to cover the difference yourself. Hence, comprehending these limits and ensuring they align with your needs is vital for effective risk management. For instance, if you have considerable assets, you might want higher liability limits to protect yourself from substantial potential losses.

Clarifying doubts with insurance agents is fundamental to ensuring clear comprehension of policy details. Agents can explain specific aspects of a policy that may not be immediately apparent. Don't hesitate to ask questions like: What exactly does this policy cover? Are there any exclusions or conditions that I should be aware of? How does filing a claim work? This interaction can uncover nuances about a policy that could significantly impact your decision. It also helps in negotiating better terms or discounts.

Engaging in thorough research and asking critical questions can empower you to make well-informed decisions. For instance, when considering auto insurance, it's advisable to look into average costs and coverage specifics, as highlighted by experts like Metz (2020). Such detailed reviews can shed light on which policies offer the best value for money, and which ones may fall short in providing comprehensive coverage.

Technology can also play a significant role in simplifying the comparison process. Various apps and online services are designed to make understanding and using insurance policies easier. These tools can offer side-by-side comparisons of different insurers, helping you identify the best option based on your specific needs. Using technology can save time and provide a clearer picture of what each insurer offers.

In addition to individual comparisons, reviewing head-to-head analyses between top insurance carriers can provide deeper insights. For example, seeing how Geico compares to Progressive in terms of coverage options and rates, or how State Farm stands against Allstate in customer satisfaction can guide your choice. Each company has its strengths and weaknesses, and understanding these can aid in selecting the most suitable policy. While USAA might excel in customer service, Progressive could offer more coverage availability, depending on your priorities *(Compare Car Insurance Rates & Shop Quotes Online (September 2023), n.d.).*

Discounts are another avenue to explore when comparing insurance options. Many insurers provide discounts for various reasons, such as bundling multiple policies, having a clean driving record, or even installing safety features in your car. These discounts can significantly reduce premiums and make a particular policy more attractive. Checking with an agent about eligible discounts and how they apply to your policy can unearth savings opportunities you might not have initially considered.

Furthermore, consider the implications of long-term commitments versus short-term gains. Sometimes, a policy might appear cheaper initially but could become more expensive over time due to gradual premium increases or insufficient coverage. Evaluating policies with a long-term perspective ensures sustained financial protection.

It's also worthwhile to understand the insurer's customer service quality and claims process. Efficient customer service and a hassle-free claims process can make a significant difference during stressful times. Research customer reviews and third-party ratings to gauge an insurer's track record in handling claims. This information can provide peace of mind knowing that support will be readily available when needed.

Avoiding Common Insurance Pitfalls

When purchasing and managing insurance, many individuals fall into common pitfalls that can leave them underinsured or paying for unnecessary coverage. This subpoint focuses on educating readers on these mistakes to help them make better-informed decisions.

One of the most prevalent errors is underinsurance. Many people believe that minimal coverage will suffice, often to save money on premiums. However, this approach can be risky. For instance, insuring your home only up to its market value instead of its replacement cost could lead to significant out-of-pocket expenses in the event of a disaster. Market value considers the land and location but doesn't adequately cover the materials and labor needed for rebuilding. To avoid gaps in coverage, it's vital to periodically reassess the value of insured assets and adjust policies accordingly. Consult with an insurance broker to ensure your coverage meets current needs.

Equally important is understanding the terms and conditions of your policies. Policyholders often overlook fine print details, which can result in unexpected issues when filing claims. For example, some policies may exclude specific types of damage, such as floods or earthquakes, requiring additional riders for comprehensive protection. Regularly reviewing policy documents helps identify any exclusions or limitations. Make it a habit to read through renewals and updates from your insurer, and don't hesitate to reach out for clarifications. Knowing precisely what your policy covers and excludes prepares you for various scenarios, ensuring you're not caught off guard.

Another critical aspect is the claims process. Efficient claim filing can make a substantial difference in how quickly and successfully your situation is resolved. Start by documenting all communications with your insurer, including phone calls, emails, and letters. Maintain copies of all relevant documents like receipts, repair estimates, and photographs of damages. Quick reporting of incidents can also expedite your claim; delaying might complicate the process or even lead to denial. Always follow the insurer's instructions carefully and provide complete information to avoid delays.

To further ease the claims process, familiarize yourself with the steps involved before an incident occurs. First, notify your insurer immediately after an event. Provide detailed accounts of what happened, accompanied by evidence if possible. Second, work with the insurer's adjuster to assess the damages accurately. Third, understand your policy's coverage limits and deductibles to know what to expect financially. By proactively managing these steps, you can ensure a smoother experience during stressful times.

Moreover, efficient claims management involves being prepared ahead of time. Create an inventory of valuable belongings with descriptions, purchase dates, and estimated values. Tools like apps or spreadsheets can help keep this information organized and accessible. When disaster strikes, having this inventory can speed up the claim process significantly.

Another common mistake is failing to update your insurance policies following significant life events. Events such as getting married, having children, moving homes, or renovating property can all impact your coverage needs. Neglecting to inform your insurer about such changes can result in underinsurance or even denied claims. Each major life change should prompt a review of your existing policies to adjust coverage levels appropriately. An updated policy ensures that new risks are adequately managed, and any potential gaps closed.

In addition to avoiding underinsurance, it's essential to recognize the risks of overinsurance. Paying for more coverage than necessary can strain your finances without providing proportional benefits. Carefully evaluate your risk factors and choose policies that balance sufficient protection with affordable premiums. If you rarely file small claims, opting for higher deductibles can reduce monthly costs, allocating those savings toward emergency funds instead. Customizing coverage based on personal circumstances can help maintain financial stability while ensuring adequate protection.

Insurance providers themselves vary in reliability and service quality. Researching an insurer's complaint record through resources like the National Association of Insurance Commissioners (NAIC) can reveal red flags regarding claim handling and customer satisfaction. Choosing a reputable provider with a track record of fair claim settlements is crucial. Bundling different types of insurance, such as auto and home, with one carrier can also offer discounts and simplified management, though it's important to compare overall benefits and costs against individual policies.

Ultimately, educating oneself on the intricacies of insurance policies and potential pitfalls empowers consumers. Understanding common mistakes doesn't just prevent financial loss; it enables informed decision-making that aligns with long-term financial goals. Effective risk management through thoughtful insurance choices safeguards your assets and peace of mind.

Key Considerations When Choosing Insurance

Understanding individual needs and matching them with suitable insurance products is fundamental when selecting the most appropriate insurance. First, assess your personal situation and recognize the unique aspects of your lifestyle that may influence your insurance requirements. For example, a young professional without dependents might prioritize health and disability insurance, while a family-oriented individual may need comprehensive life and health insurance.

Assessing policy features and benefits to align with long-term financial goals is another critical step. Each insurance product comes with distinct features such as coverage limits, exclusions, and premium structures. It's essential to evaluate these elements in the context of your financial objectives. If your goal is to ensure your child's education is funded in case of unexpected events, you might consider a term life insurance policy with high coverage for an extended period. Conversely, if you're looking at long-term wealth accumulation along with protection, whole life or universal life insurance might be more suitable.

Additionally, it's crucial to understand how specific policies can tie into other aspects of your financial plan. For instance, some life insurance policies offer investment components that grow over time, providing both death benefits and potential savings growth. Integrating such a policy with your retirement planning can offer additional security and financial flexibility.

Evaluating an insurer's customer service and support for future claims handling is also vital. An insurance policy is only as good as the company's ability to honor it when needed. Research the insurer's reputation through customer reviews, ratings from independent agencies, and financial stability indicators. Companies with a strong track record in processing claims efficiently and offering robust customer support can provide peace of mind and confidence in times of need.

Consider reaching out to current policyholders or consulting independent review sites to gather insights on the insurer's responsiveness and effectiveness in claim management. This information can be invaluable in avoiding frustrations and delays should you ever need to file a claim.

Considering affordability and balancing premiums with coverage requirements ensures that the chosen policy is sustainable in the long term. While it's tempting to opt for maximum coverage, it's important to select a policy whose premiums fit comfortably within your budget. Striking a balance between adequate coverage and affordable premiums prevents scenarios where you might have to cancel a policy due to financial strain.

To determine the right balance, start by evaluating your monthly income and expenses. Allocate a specific portion of your budget for insurance premiums, ensuring they don't compromise your ability to meet other financial obligations. Tools like online calculators and consultations with insurance professionals can help estimate appropriate coverage levels based on your financial position.

Affordability also ties into understanding the trade-offs between different types of policies. For instance, term life insurance typically offers higher coverage at lower premiums compared to whole life insurance. However, term policies expire after a set period, potentially leaving you uninsured later in life. Weighing these differences against your long-term goals and current financial capacity will guide you in making a prudent choice.

When considering long-term affordability, also account for potential changes in your financial situation. Life events such as marriage, the birth of a child, or career advancements can alter your insurance needs and ability to pay premiums. Selecting a flexible policy that allows adjustments to coverage amounts or payment terms can help accommodate these changes without needing to switch insurers or obtain new policies.

By understanding individual needs and matching them with suitable insurance products, assessing policy features and benefits to align with long-term financial goals, evaluating an insurer's customer service and claims handling, and considering affordability and balancing premiums with coverage requirements, you'll be well-equipped to make informed decisions about your insurance needs.

Concluding Thoughts

In this chapter, we have delved into the various types of insurance available and their roles in effective risk management. Health, auto, home, and life insurance each serve unique purposes, offering protection against different risks that can lead to significant financial loss. Understanding the specifics of each type of coverage, from employer-sponsored health plans to homeowner's policies that guard against property damage, helps individuals make informed decisions tailored to their needs. By evaluating personal circumstances and choosing appropriate insurance options, one can better safeguard against unforeseen events.

As we conclude, it's clear that having a comprehensive understanding of insurance types is fundamental to managing potential risks effectively. This knowledge empowers individuals to assess their own situations, weigh the necessity of different coverages, and select policies that provide adequate protection without overspending. By doing so, working professionals and those aiming for financial freedom can ensure they are well-protected, maintaining financial stability even in the face of unexpected challenges.

Alex Knight

Chapter 10 : Building Wealth: A Long-Term Perspective

Building wealth requires a long-term perspective that prioritizes sustainable strategies and financial independence. This chapter delves into the fundamental aspects of wealth-building, emphasizing methods that harness the power of time and patience to generate substantial financial growth. Avoiding the allure of quick wins, it steers readers toward approaches that promise stability and gradual accumulation of assets. By understanding these foundational principles, individuals can better position themselves to achieve their financial goals and leave a meaningful legacy.

Throughout this chapter, readers will explore various strategies designed to maximize wealth over the long term. Key topics include the profound impact of compound interest, which exemplifies how small, consistent investments can grow exponentially over decades. The discussion will also cover diverse investment vehicles such as high-yield savings accounts, stocks, and mutual funds, each offering unique opportunities for compounding returns. Additionally, practical advice on investing during market downturns will highlight the resilience of long-term strategies. Educating future generations about these concepts ensures that the knowledge and benefits of smart investing are passed down, reinforcing the importance of financial literacy in achieving lasting wealth.

The Power of Compound Interest

Compound interest is a powerful tool that can dramatically impact wealth accumulation over time. Understanding how it works and leveraging its potential are crucial steps in building long-term financial security.

To begin with, compound interest grows exponentially over time. This concept may seem abstract at first, but imagine a snowball rolling down a hill. It starts small but gathers more snow as it continues rolling, growing bigger and faster. Similarly, with compound interest, the initial investment earns interest, and then that earned interest also generates further interest, leading to exponential growth. The key to maximizing this exponential growth lies in starting early. For example, if you invest $1,000 at an annual interest rate of 5%, compounded monthly, your investment would grow to $1,647.67 over ten years. The earlier you start investing, the more time your money has to capitalize on the "interest-on-interest" effect, resulting in significantly larger returns.

Investing in assets with higher compounding potential can further amplify wealth growth. Not all investments yield the same returns, and varying assets come with different compounding frequencies and rates. High-yield savings accounts, certificates of deposit (CDs), stocks, and mutual funds are examples of investments with potentially higher compounding returns. As a practical illustration, consider two types of investments: one yielding simple interest and another with compound interest. If you invest $100,000 in an asset that offers 8% simple interest annually for 20 years, you would end up with $260,000. However, if that interest compounds monthly, the ending balance would be nearly $493,000. Clearly, compound interest is much more lucrative over the long term. Therefore, seeking investments with favorable compounding characteristics can significantly boost your overall wealth accumulation (*The Power of Compound Interest: Secrets to Long-Term Wealth Building, 2024*).

Long-term investors benefit from the smoothing effect of compounding, even during market downturns. Market fluctuations and economic downturns are inevitable; however, the power of compound interest can help mitigate the adverse effects over time. During a market downturn, the lower prices of assets can still benefit from reinvested interest or dividends, allowing the portfolio to recover and even thrive as the market rebounds. For instance, during the 2008 financial crisis, many portfolios suffered substantial losses. Yet, those who continued to invest and reinvest their earnings, riding out the market downturn, often saw their portfolios regain value and continue to grow once the market recovered. This illustrates the resilience and long-term benefits of compound interest, reinforcing the importance of maintaining a patient and long-term perspective on investments. By staying invested and taking advantage of compounding, investors can achieve steady growth despite short-term market volatility (*Understanding Compound Interest Can Help You Grow Wealth, n.d.*).

Educating descendants about compound interest empowers them to continue the wealth-building legacy. Financial literacy is a valuable skill that can be passed down through generations, ensuring that the principles of smart investing and the benefits of compound interest are well understood. Teaching children and young adults about the basics of compound interest, how it works, and why it's important can set them on a path toward financial independence. Simple activities like setting up a high-yield savings account for a child or involving them in discussions about family investments can provide hands-on learning experiences. Providing educational resources and encouraging continuous learning about personal finance can further solidify these principles. For example, a parent might show their teenager how a small monthly investment, combined with compound interest, can grow into a significant sum over decades, motivating them to start saving early and consistently.

Additionally, incorporating practical strategies such as automated contributions into their routines can make a considerable difference. By automating regular contributions to savings or investment accounts, individuals can ensure steady growth without needing to remember to make manual deposits. This 'set it and forget it' approach not only simplifies the process but also guarantees consistent investment, which is crucial for maximizing the benefits of compound interest.

Moreover, employing tools like the Rule of 72 can make the concept of compound interest more tangible. The Rule of 72 is a straightforward way to estimate how long it will take for an investment to double given a fixed annual rate of return. Simply divide 72 by the annual interest rate to get the approximate number of years needed for doubling the initial investment. For example, at an 8% annual return, it will take around nine years for the investment to double. Utilizing such tools can demystify compound interest and empower individuals to make informed financial decisions confidently.

Real Estate Investing

Real estate has long been heralded as a cornerstone of wealth-building strategies, offering numerous avenues for financial growth. Exploring real estate as an asset class reveals several strategies for successful investment, each with its unique benefits and challenges.

Strategic property selection is paramount in driving substantial value appreciation over time. Investors must focus on high-growth areas, which often exhibit robust economic development, increasing job opportunities, and a rising population. These factors create demand for housing, thereby pushing property values upward. Researching urban development plans, transportation projects, and local economic indicators can help investors pinpoint such high-growth areas. For example, cities undergoing revitalization or expansion often present lucrative opportunities. In these regions, early investments can yield significant returns as development progresses, transforming the area into a desirable and valuable location.

Owning and renting out properties serves as another effective strategy for wealth accumulation. Rental properties provide a steady stream of income, supplementing other financial gains. This consistent cash flow can be particularly beneficial for investors seeking to diversify their income sources. Managing rental properties, however, requires diligence and a thorough understanding of tenant management, maintenance, and local rental laws. Successful landlords often adopt practices that include regular property maintenance, clear communication with tenants, and prompt resolution of issues to ensure tenant satisfaction and minimize vacancies. Additionally, employing experienced property managers can help streamline operations, allowing investors to focus on expanding their portfolios.

Tax benefits associated with real estate investing offer another compelling reason for its inclusion in a wealth-building strategy. Deductions for mortgage interest, property taxes, and depreciation can significantly lower tax liabilities, enhancing overall returns. For instance, depreciation allows investors to deduct a portion of the property's cost from their taxable income, even as the property potentially appreciates in value. Understanding and leveraging these deductions requires staying informed about current tax laws and regulations. Consulting with a tax professional ensures compliance and maximizes available benefits, making real estate a tax-advantageous investment option.

Moreover, real estate investments can provide a safeguard against market volatility prevalent in other asset classes, such as stocks or bonds. While financial markets can fluctuate widely based on various economic factors, real estate tends to offer more stability. Physical properties are tangible assets whose value generally doesn't experience the same level of daily fluctuations as securities. This relative stability makes real estate an attractive component in a diversified investment portfolio. By balancing real estate with other investments, investors can mitigate risks associated with market downturns, ultimately contributing to a more resilient financial foundation.

Beyond individual properties, diverse investment vehicles within the real estate sector further enhance wealth-building potential. Real Estate Investment Trusts (REITs) allow individuals to invest in large-scale, income-producing real estate without directly owning properties. REITs distribute a significant portion of their income as dividends, providing investors with regular payouts akin to those from direct property ownership but without the hassle of property management. Additionally, REITs offer liquidity similar to stocks, enabling investors to buy and sell shares easily. This flexibility makes REITs an accessible and attractive option for those looking to gain exposure to real estate without committing to property purchases.

Another avenue to consider is real estate crowdfunding platforms, which pool resources from multiple investors to fund real estate projects. This model democratizes access to real estate investments, allowing individuals to invest smaller amounts in larger developments. Crowdfunding can target various types of real estate, including commercial, residential, and mixed-use properties, each presenting different risk and return profiles. While offering diversification benefits, it's important for investors to conduct thorough due diligence on the platform and the specific projects to assess their viability and potential returns.

Furthermore, house flipping—buying properties, renovating them, and selling at a profit—can be a highly lucrative strategy when executed correctly. Success in house flipping hinges on accurately assessing renovation costs, effectively managing projects within budget, and timing the market to sell at peak value. This approach demands a keen eye for undervalued properties and potential improvements that can significantly enhance market appeal. Networking with contractors, real estate agents, and inspectors can aid in identifying suitable projects and carrying out renovations efficiently.

Regardless of the chosen strategy, identifying and managing risk is a crucial aspect of real estate investing. Market conditions, property-specific issues, and broader economic trends all influence real estate values and returns. Investors should undertake comprehensive market analysis, including studying historical trends, vacancy rates, and future development plans to better understand potential risks and rewards. Diversifying across different property types and geographic locations can also mitigate risk by reducing the impact of localized market downturns.

Additionally, it's essential to incorporate a long-term perspective when planning real estate investments. Real estate generally appreciates over time, especially when maintained well and strategically located. Patience and disciplined holding periods enable investors to ride out short-term market fluctuations, ultimately reaping significant gains. Integrating real estate into a broader financial plan, encompassing other investments and retirement goals, ensures a balanced and sustainable approach to wealth building.

Legacy Planning

Legacy planning is a critical component in building and preserving wealth for future generations. It ensures that the hard-earned assets you've accumulated over your lifetime are managed, distributed, and used in ways that reflect your values and intentions. This process involves several important steps and considerations, which we'll explore through various aspects of legacy planning.

Drafting a will and establishing trusts are foundational elements of legacy planning. A will is a legal document that specifies how your assets should be distributed after your death. It allows you to name executors who will manage your estate, appoint guardians for minor children, and state your final wishes regarding asset distribution. On the other hand, a trust is a fiduciary arrangement that enables a trustee to hold and manage assets on behalf of beneficiaries. Trusts can offer significant advantages, such as avoiding probate, minimizing estate taxes, and protecting assets from creditors. For example, a revocable living trust lets you maintain control over your assets during your lifetime and provides flexibility to make changes as needed. In contrast, an irrevocable trust offers greater protection against estate taxes but limits your ability to modify its terms.

Establishing family meetings and councils is another essential strategy in legacy planning. These gatherings bring family members together to discuss wealth management, shared values, and future goals. By creating a structured environment for open communication, families can address potential conflicts and ensure a unified approach to managing and preserving wealth. These meetings can also serve as educational sessions where younger generations learn about financial planning, investment strategies, and the responsibilities that come with inheriting wealth. For example, a family council might meet quarterly to review financial statements, discuss philanthropic activities, and plan for future investments. This involvement fosters a sense of responsibility and prepares heirs to manage their inheritance wisely.

Incorporating charitable giving into your legacy plan aligns with family values and creates a lasting legacy of giving back. Philanthropy allows you to support causes and initiatives that are meaningful to you while potentially reducing estate taxes. There are several ways to include charitable giving in your estate plan. One option is to establish a charitable trust, such as a charitable remainder trust, which provides income to beneficiaries for a specified period before donating the remaining assets to a charity. Another option is to create a donor-advised fund, allowing you to make a charitable contribution and receive an immediate tax deduction while recommending grants to your favorite charities over time. Naming charities as beneficiaries of specific assets or a percentage of your estate is also a viable option. This approach not only benefits society but also instills a sense of philanthropy in future generations.

Identifying and grooming successors within the family is crucial for sustaining the business's continuity and legacy. This aspect of legacy planning involves selecting and preparing individuals to take over leadership roles and manage family assets effectively. Succession planning ensures that the next generation is ready to handle the financial responsibilities and challenges that come with inherited wealth. It may involve mentoring, training programs, and gradual transitions to leadership roles. For instance, a family business owner might start by involving their children in small projects or decision-making processes, gradually increasing their responsibilities over time. This hands-on experience helps successors develop the skills and confidence needed to lead successfully.

Creating a comprehensive legacy plan requires careful consideration and professional guidance. Estate planning attorneys, financial advisors, and other experts can help you navigate the complexities of legacy planning, ensuring that your wishes are accurately documented and legally binding. These professionals can assist in exploring various strategies, such as setting up trusts, life insurance policies, and tax-efficient gifting options. They can also help evaluate different types of trusts to determine which best suits your needs and goals. For example, a financial advisor might recommend an irrevocable life insurance trust to minimize estate taxes and provide liquidity for estate settlement costs.

Family governance structures play a vital role in preserving wealth and values across generations. Setting up a family governance structure involves creating a family constitution, defining roles and responsibilities, and establishing guidelines for decision-making processes. This structure helps ensure that the family's wealth and values are preserved as they pass down through the generations. It also provides a framework for resolving conflicts and making collective decisions about investments, spending, and philanthropic activities. For example, a family constitution might outline the family's mission, vision, and core values, along with specific rules for managing family businesses and assets.

Education and mentorship are integral components of legacy planning. Passing down knowledge, skills, and experiences to future generations empowers them to make informed decisions and manage inherited wealth responsibly. One effective strategy is to establish educational funds or trusts that support the educational aspirations of your children, grandchildren, or other beneficiaries. These funds can cover tuition fees, provide access to educational resources, or support mentorship programs. Additionally, involving younger family members in financial discussions and decision-making processes helps them understand the complexities of wealth management and prepares them for future responsibilities.

Open and honest communication within the family is essential for successful legacy planning. Transparent discussions about wealth, values, and expectations help prevent misunderstandings and conflicts. It's important to involve family members in the planning process, allowing them to voice their opinions and concerns. This collaborative approach fosters understanding, unity, and a sense of shared responsibility. For example, holding regular family meetings to discuss the legacy plan and address any questions or issues that arise ensures that everyone is on the same page and committed to the family's long-term goals.

Continuous Education and Adaptation

Continuous learning and adaptability are critical components in successful wealth-building strategies. In an ever-evolving financial landscape, individuals who prioritize education and remain flexible in their approach are far more likely to achieve long-term financial independence.

One effective way to enhance financial literacy and investment skills is by attending seminars, workshops, and courses. These educational opportunities can provide valuable insights and up-to-date information on various aspects of personal finance and investing. For instance, a workshop on the latest tax regulations could help you identify new ways to optimize your tax strategy, while a course on stock market analysis might give you the tools to make better investment decisions. Such events often feature experts in the field who can offer practical advice and answer specific questions related to your financial situation. Moreover, these settings provide a platform for networking with like-minded individuals, which can lead to valuable connections and collaborations.

Another essential practice in wealth-building is reassessing your investment allocations and asset allocations based on changing market conditions. The financial markets are dynamic, influenced by factors such as economic indicators, geopolitical events, and technological advancements. By periodically reviewing and adjusting your portfolio, you ensure that your investments remain aligned with your financial goals and risk tolerance. For example, during a market downturn, you might decide to shift some of your assets from stocks to bonds to reduce risk. Conversely, in a booming market, you might take on a bit more risk to capitalize on potential gains. Continual reassessment helps protect your investments from significant losses and positions you to take advantage of emerging opportunities.

Establishing a trusted advisory team is another key element in building wealth. A team comprising financial advisors, tax professionals, and estate planners can offer specialized expertise tailored to your individual needs. Financial advisors can help you develop a comprehensive investment strategy, while tax professionals can provide insight into minimizing tax liabilities. Estate planners can assist in creating a plan to manage your assets and pass them on to future generations. Having a knowledgeable and trusted advisor is particularly beneficial, as they can guide you through complex financial decisions and help you stay on track to meet your long-term objectives. According to Grimm, obtaining special certifications such as retirement income planning or long-term care planning can significantly enhance the services provided by an advisor (Grimm, 2024).

Diversifying investments and implementing risk mitigation strategies are also crucial for protecting against potential losses. Diversification involves spreading investments across various asset classes, industries, and geographic regions to reduce exposure to any single risk. While one sector may experience a downturn, another might be performing well, balancing out overall portfolio performance. Additionally, employing risk mitigation strategies such as setting stop-loss orders, using hedging techniques, and maintaining a cash reserve can further safeguard your investments. By diversifying and managing risk effectively, you can navigate market fluctuations more confidently and preserve your capital over the long term.

Incorporating continuous learning into your financial strategy involves staying informed about the latest trends, tools, and strategies in the financial sector. One practical approach is to engage with industry publications, white papers, and podcasts. These resources offer a wealth of knowledge and can keep you updated on current developments. For instance, reading financial journals can provide insights into emerging investment opportunities, while tuning into podcasts by industry leaders can help you understand complex financial concepts in a more accessible format. Continuous education empowers you to make informed decisions, adapt to market changes, and ultimately achieve your financial goals.

Furthermore, increasing financial literacy doesn't end with formal education; it extends to everyday practices such as monitoring your investments regularly and staying aware of market news. Tools and technologies like financial apps and online dashboards make it easier than ever to keep track of your portfolio's performance. Regularly reviewing your investments allows you to make timely adjustments and ensure that your strategy remains aligned with your financial objectives. Staying abreast of market news helps you anticipate changes that could affect your investments and prepare accordingly.

Networking with other investors and financial professionals can also provide valuable learning opportunities. Joining investment clubs, participating in online forums, or attending industry conferences allows you to share experiences, discuss strategies, and gain different perspectives. These interactions can introduce you to new ideas and approaches that you may not have considered. Moreover, networking can lead to mentorship opportunities where experienced investors can offer guidance and support as you navigate your financial journey.

Adopting a mindset of lifelong learning is vital for sustained wealth-building. It involves being proactive in seeking out new information, staying curious, and being open to adapting your strategies as needed. This approach not only helps you stay ahead of the curve but also builds resilience against unforeseen challenges. As markets evolve and new investment products and technologies emerge, those who continuously educate themselves will be better positioned to take advantage of these changes and grow their wealth.

Maximizing Returns

Making informed investment decisions to maximize returns is crucial for building wealth over the long term. One effective strategy for doing this is investing in assets with higher compounding potential. Compounding has a profound impact on wealth growth, as it allows your investments to generate earnings not only on the original amount invested but also on the accumulated returns from previous periods.

Investing in assets that offer a higher rate of return can significantly accelerate the growth of your portfolio. For example, stocks are known for their potential to provide higher returns compared to other asset classes like bonds or savings accounts. Companies that pay dividends and have a history of increasing those dividends over time are particularly attractive. Reinvesting these dividends enables you to buy more shares, thereby creating a cycle of continuous growth. According to Hartford Funds, dividend reinvestment can account for up to 90% of the total return of the S&P 500 over long periods *(Compounding Dividends: The Secret Sauce to Growing Your Portfolio, n.d.).*

Regular reinvestment of dividends and interest can further boost overall returns. By reinvesting your earnings back into your investment portfolio, you effectively increase your holdings without needing additional capital. This practice enhances the compounding effect, which is instrumental in wealth accumulation. For instance, an investor who consistently reinvests dividends will see their portfolio grow at an accelerating rate due to the increased number of shares yielding dividends.

Long-term investors benefit significantly from the smoothing effect of compounding, even during market downturns. Market volatility is a natural part of investing, and while it can be unsettling, taking a long-term perspective helps mitigate its impact. Over time, the effects of short-term market fluctuations tend to even out, allowing the compounding gains to take center stage. A notable example is the investment strategy of Warren Buffett, who has consistently emphasized the importance of a long-term approach and the power of compounding. Buffett's investments, based on solid companies and reinvested returns, have generated substantial wealth over decades.

Creating generational wealth through the knowledge of compound interest ensures a lasting financial legacy. Teaching future generations about the power of compounding and the importance of starting early can have a profound impact on their financial future. For instance, Ronald Read, a janitor and gas station attendant, amassed a stock portfolio worth millions through diligent saving and investing in blue-chip, dividend-paying stocks. His success story illustrates that even individuals with modest beginnings can achieve significant wealth through compounding.

Parents and guardians can play a pivotal role in this educational process by establishing investment accounts for their children and explaining the principles of compound interest. By demonstrating how small, regular investments can grow substantially over time, they instill valuable financial habits that can last a lifetime. Tools such as custodial accounts or 529 education savings plans can be effective vehicles for this purpose, providing both financial growth and educational opportunities for the next generation.

In addition to individual stocks, other investment vehicles like mutual funds, exchange-traded funds (ETFs), and real estate can also offer substantial compounding potential. Mutual funds and ETFs, for instance, provide diversification across various asset classes and sectors, which helps spread risk while maintaining the potential for high returns. Real estate investments, when strategically selected and held long-term, can appreciate in value and generate rental income, both of which contribute to wealth growth.

Regularly reviewing and adjusting one's investment portfolio is essential for maximizing returns. As market conditions and personal financial goals evolve, so should your investment strategy. Ensuring that you maintain a diversified portfolio tailored to your risk tolerance and investment horizon is crucial. Diversification reduces the risk of significant losses from any single investment and allows for smoother overall portfolio performance.

Utilizing tax-efficient investment strategies can also enhance wealth growth. Tax-advantaged accounts like Roth IRAs or 401(k) plans allow earnings to grow tax-free or tax-deferred. This means that the compounding effect is not diminished by yearly taxes, thereby accelerating growth. Furthermore, being mindful of capital gains taxes and strategically taking advantage of tax-loss harvesting can optimize after-tax returns.

Education plays a critical role in making informed investment decisions. Continuously learning about financial markets, staying updated with economic trends, and understanding different investment products can empower investors to make better choices. Whether through books, online courses, seminars, or the advice of financial advisors, gaining knowledge ensures that investors are equipped to navigate the complexities of the financial world effectively.

Moreover, setting clear financial goals and developing a robust investment plan aligned with those goals is essential. A well-defined plan provides direction and keeps investors focused on long-term objectives, rather than being swayed by short-term market movements. It involves assessing risk tolerance, determining asset allocation, and periodically rebalancing the portfolio to stay on track with the intended investment strategy.

Final Thoughts

Understanding the power of compound interest and its long-term benefits is essential for anyone seeking financial independence. This chapter has emphasized the importance of starting early to maximize exponential growth, as even small investments can yield significant returns over time. By choosing assets with higher compounding potential and reinvesting earnings, wealth can grow steadily despite market fluctuations. The resilience provided by compound interest during downturns highlights the value of maintaining a patient and disciplined approach to investing.

Equally important is passing on this knowledge to future generations, ensuring they too can benefit from smart financial strategies. Educating children and young adults about compound interest fosters a legacy of financial literacy and independence, equipping them with the tools needed for prosperous futures. Practical strategies like automating contributions and utilizing tools such as the Rule of 72 can further simplify the investment process, making it easier for everyone to harness the full potential of compound interest.

Alex Knight

conclusion

The journey through financial literacy and effective money management is one that can transform your life. Throughout this book, we have explored the fundamental elements necessary for understanding and mastering personal finance, transforming what often feels like an overwhelming topic into a series of manageable steps. Each chapter has been dedicated to equipping you with the knowledge and tools needed to take control of your financial destiny.

Starting with the essentials, we examined how critical it is to grasp the basics of financial literacy. This foundation serves as the bedrock upon which all other financial knowledge is built. By understanding concepts like income, expenses, assets, and liabilities, you've taken the first step towards informed decision-making regarding your finances. Recognizing these core elements helps demystify money management and sets the stage for more advanced strategies.

We then delved into the art of setting financial goals. These goals are your roadmap to success, guiding your decisions and helping you prioritize where your money should go. We've discussed the importance of making these goals clear and achievable, ensuring they are realistic and tailored to your personal situation. Whether it's saving for a down payment on a house, paying off student loans, or planning for retirement, having specific targets keeps you motivated and focused.

Creating and maintaining a practical budget was another crucial lesson. Budgeting is not about restricting yourself but about gaining awareness and control over your spending. With a solid budget, you can see exactly where your money is going and make adjustments to ensure you're living within your means. This practice is key to avoiding debt and saving for future needs.

Speaking of saving, we emphasized the significance of building a robust savings plan. Establishing an emergency fund, saving for major purchases, and consistently setting aside funds for retirement are all vital components of a sound financial strategy. The discipline of saving regularly cannot be overstated – it's the cornerstone of financial stability and security.

Investing wisely is another pillar of financial health. We covered different investment vehicles, risk tolerance, and the importance of diversifying your portfolio. Investing isn't just for the wealthy; it's a powerful tool for anyone looking to grow their wealth over time. Understanding market dynamics, compound interest, and long-term growth can help you make informed decisions that align with your financial goals.

Debt management is an area many struggle with, so we addressed strategies for effectively handling debt. From consolidating loans to negotiating interest rates and creating a repayment plan, there are several ways to manage and reduce debt. The aim is to free up resources that can be redirected towards savings and investments, thus improving your overall financial health.

Increasing your income streams was another topic of focus. We highlighted various methods to boost earnings, such as side hustles, passive income opportunities, and advancing in your career. By diversifying your income sources, you create additional security and accelerate your journey towards financial independence.

Planning for retirement may seem distant, but starting early can significantly impact your future comfort. We discussed different retirement accounts, contribution strategies, and the power of compounding interest. Being proactive about retirement planning ensures you can enjoy your later years without financial stress.

Additionally, choosing the right insurance plays a crucial role in protecting your assets and providing peace of mind. From health to life insurance, having adequate coverage is essential in safeguarding against unforeseen events that could otherwise derail your financial plans.

Long-term wealth-building strategies tie all these elements together, focusing on sustaining and growing your wealth over time. We explored avenues like real estate, entrepreneurship, and leveraging technology to build a diversified and resilient financial portfolio.

As you reflect on these lessons, it's important to remember that financial literacy is not a one-time achievement but an ongoing process. Continue educating yourself, stay curious, and seek out new information. Take small steps each day towards your financial goals, track your progress, and don't shy away from asking for help when needed. Financial well-being is a continuous journey, and every bit of effort counts.

In light of everything you've learned, it's time to take action. You now have a wealth of knowledge and practical strategies at your disposal. Use them to make informed decisions, set priorities, and work diligently towards financial empowerment. Take charge of your financial future by making choices that align with your long-term objectives, seeking opportunities to increase your income, and always keeping an eye on your financial security.

Finally, I want to extend my deepest gratitude to you. Thank you for dedicating your time and energy to learning about financial literacy and money management. Your commitment to understanding these important principles will surely lead to a more secure and prosperous financial future. Keep striving, stay focused, and trust in your ability to achieve financial success. Wishing you all the best as you apply these strategies and continue your journey towards financial independence and empowerment.

Reference List

Budgeting and Goal Setting | Financial Literacy. (n.d.). Finlit.yale.edu. https://finlit.yale.edu/planning/budgeting-and-goal-setting

Budgeting. (n.d.). Washington State Department of Financial Institutions. https://dfi.wa.gov/financial-education/information/budgeting

Budgeting and Personal Financial Planning Skills - MAU. (n.d.). Www.maufl.edu. https://www.maufl.edu/en/news-and-events/macaws-blog/budgeting-and-personal-financial-planning-skills

Cruze, R. (2022, April 25). *How to Set Financial Goals.* Ramsey Solutions. https://www.ramseysolutions.com/personal-growth/setting-financial-goals

Holzhauer, B. (2021, May 26). *The Best Budgeting Apps Of June 2021.* Forbes Advisor. https://www.forbes.com/advisor/banking/best-budgeting-apps/

How to Choose the Right Budget System. (n.d.). NerdWallet. https://www.nerdwallet.com/article/finance/how-to-choose-the-right-budget-system

O'Neill, B. (2017, June). *The Benefits of Budgeting (Rutgers NJAES).* Njaes.rutgers.edu.

https://njaes.rutgers.edu/sshw/message/message.php?p=Finance&m=351

The 5 Most Effective Budgeting Methods — and How to Use Them. (2024). Nasdaq.com. https://www.nasdaq.com/articles/the-5-most-effective-budgeting-methods-and-how-to-use-them

The Best Personal Finance Software for 2022. (n.d.). PCMAG. https://www.pcmag.com/picks/the-best-personal-finance-services

Why Budgeting Is Important (Even If You're Wealthy). (n.d.). Smartasset.com. https://smartasset.com/personal-finance/why-is-budgeting-so-important

7 Best High-Yield Online Savings Accounts of December 2021. (n.d.). NerdWallet. https://www.nerdwallet.com/best/banking/high-yield-online-savings-accounts

Appleby, D. (2019). *10 Tips for Achieving Financial Security*. Investopedia. https://www.investopedia.com/articles/retirement/06/10securerretirementtips.asp

Best High-Yield Savings Accounts Of October 2022 – Forbes Advisor. (n.d.). Www.forbes.com. https://www.forbes.com/advisor/banking/savings/best-high-yield-savings-accounts/

Binger, C. (2023, July 3). *4 Benefits of Automating Savings*. Embark Financial Partners. https://embarkfp.com/4-benefits-of-automating-savings/

Emergency Savings. (n.d.). Commonwealth. https://buildcommonwealth.org/our-work/emergency-savings/

Four Reasons Emergency Funds are Important › 1st United Credit Union. (n.d.). Www.1stunitedcu.org. https://www.1stunitedcu.org/more-for-you/financial-wellness/four-reasons-emergency-funds-are-important

How to save money. (n.d.). Fortune Recommends. https://fortune.com/recommends/banking/how-to-save-money/

Sinking Funds Help Handle Expenses, Avoid Debt. (2022, March 14). NerdWallet. https://www.nerdwallet.com/article/finance/nerdwallet-sinking-fund-savings

What Is a Sinking Fund and How Do You Create One? (n.d.). Ramsey Solutions. https://www.ramseysolutions.com/saving/stop-the-panic-sinking-fund

Zhyliaev, V. (2023, September 25). *What are the advantages of automating my savings?* Medium. https://volodymyrzh.medium.com/what-are-the-advantages-of-automating-my-savings-6e459c1ee037?source=rss-------1

Ashworth, W. (2023, July 26). *6 Common Portfolio Protection Strategies*. Investopedia. https://www.investopedia.com/articles/basics/11/5-portfolio-protection-strategies.asp

Allison, D. (2022, July 12). *4 Steps To Creating a Better Investment Strategy*. Investopedia. https://www.investopedia.com/articles/trading/10/creating-a-better-investment-strategy.asp

Cote, C. (2022, June 16). *Time Value of Money (TVM): A Primer*. Harvard Business School. https://online.hbs.edu/blog/post/time-value-of-money

Diversification in Investing May Reduce Risk | U.S. Bank. (2020, October 22). Www.usbank.com. https://www.usbank.com/investing/financial-perspectives/investing-insights/diversification-important-in-investing-because.html

Geier, B. (2023, June 21). *11 Common Types of Investments and How They Work*. SmartAsset. https://smartasset.com/investing/types-of-investment

Hofstrand, D. (2023, March). *Understanding the Time Value of Money | Ag Decision Maker*. Www.extension.iastate.edu. https://www.extension.iastate.edu/agdm/wholefarm/html/c5-96.html

Lioudis, N. (2022). *The Importance Of Diversification*. Investopedia. https://www.investopedia.com/investing/importance-diversification/

Picardo, E. (2022, July 22). *Investing Explained: Types of Investments and How To Get Started*. Investopedia. https://www.investopedia.com/terms/i/investing.asp

Risk & Return: You Can't Have One Without the Other | Texas State Securities Board. (n.d.). Ssb.texas.gov. https://ssb.texas.gov/risk-return-you-cant-have-one-without-other

Segal, T. (2022, October 29). *Is There a Positive Correlation Between Risk and Return?* Investopedia. https://www.investopedia.com/ask/answers/040715/there-positive-correlation-between-risk-and-return.asp

Alexandrov, A., Brown, A., & Jain –, S. (2023, July 26). *Looking at credit scores only tells part of the story – cashflow data may tell another part.* Consumer Financial Protection Bureau. https://www.consumerfinance.gov/about-us/blog/credit-scores-only-tells-part-of-the-story-cashflow-data/

Budgeting and Personal Financial Planning Skills - MAU. (n.d.). Www.maufl.edu. https://www.maufl.edu/en/news-and-events/macaws-blog/budgeting-and-personal-financial-planning-skills

Curtis, T. (2023, April 10). *Pay Off Debt: Tools and Tips.* NerdWallet. https://www.nerdwallet.com/article/finance/pay-off-debt

Dean, L. T., & Nicholas, L. H. (2018, November). *Using Credit Scores to Understand Predictors and Consequences of Disease.* American Journal of Public Health. https://doi.org/10.2105/ajph.2018.304705

Financial Literacy and Budgeting. (n.d.). Www.csmd.edu. https://www.csmd.edu/costs-aid/financial-literacy/index.html

Health Care Debt In The U.S.: The Broad Consequences Of Medical And Dental Bills - Main Findings - 9957 | KFF. (2024, February 13). KFF. https://outreach.senate.gov/iqextranet/iqClickTrk.aspx?&cid=SenSanders&crop=21128.107075904.12578904.731960744&report_id=&redirect=https%3A%2F%2Fwww.kff.org%2Freport-section%2Fkff-health-care-debt-survey-main-findings%2F&redir_log=099897788104538

Steinberg, S., & Snider, S. (2019). *10 Easy Ways to Pay Off Debt*. US News & World Report; U.S. News & World Report. https://money.usnews.com/money/personal-finance/debt/articles/easy-ways-to-pay-off-debt

Sweet, E., Nandi, A., Adam, E. K., & McDade, T. W. (2013, August). *The high price of debt: Household financial debt and its impact on mental and physical health*. Social Science & Medicine. https://doi.org/10.1016/j.socscimed.2013.05.009

Three Steps to Managing and Getting Out of Debt. (2024, April 23). The Department of Financial Protection and Innovation. https://dfpi.ca.gov/2024/04/23/three-steps-to-managing-and-getting-out-of-debt/

https://www.facebook.com/CFPB. (2019, April 3). *Need help with your credit card debt? Start with your credit card company!* Consumer Financial Protection Bureau. https://www.consumerfinance.gov/about-us/blog/need-help-your-credit-card-debt-start-your-credit-card-company/

9 Ways to Boost Your Social Security Benefits. (2019). Investopedia. https://www.investopedia.com/articles/retirement/112116/10-social-security-secrets-could-boost-your-benefits.asp

Best Retirement Calculator (2019) - See How Much You'll Need | SmartAsset.com. (2019). SmartAsset. https://smartasset.com/retirement/retirement-calculator

GAO-11-400, Retirement Income: Ensuring Income throughout Retirement Requires Difficult Choices. (n.d.). Www.gao.gov. Retrieved July 21, 2024, from https://www.gao.gov/assets/a319390.html

How to plan for rising health care costs | Fidelity. (2019). Fidelity.com. https://www.fidelity.com/viewpoints/personal-finance/plan-for-rising-health-care-costs

Hartman, R., & Marquardt, K. (2023). *Great Retirement Planning Tools and Software for 2023. US News & World Report*. Retrieved from https://money.usnews.com/money/retirement/401ks/articles/best-retirement-planning-tools-and-software

Inc, F. B. F. L. F. T. D. A. is the C. of A. R. C., Books, C.-A. of S., Thous, P. T. to, & Appleby, s of professionals L. about our editorial policies D. (n.d.). *The Best Retirement Plans*. Investopedia. https://www.investopedia.com/articles/retirement/08/best-plan.asp

Kagan, J. (2022, January 3). *Individual Retirement Account (IRA)*. Investopedia. https://www.investopedia.com/terms/i/ira.asp

Lake, R. (2023, October 23). *How to plan for medical expenses in retirement*. Investopedia. https://www.investopedia.com/retirement/how-plan-medical-expenses-retirement/

Portfolio Theory, Life-Cycle Investing, and Retirement Income. (2007, October). Social Security Administration Research, Statistics, and Policy Analysis. https://www.ssa.gov/policy/docs/policybriefs/pb2007-02.html

inFeatures, J. "JB" B. published. (2024, April 18). *Strategies to Optimize Your Social Security Benefits*. Kiplinger.com. https://www.kiplinger.com/retirement/social-security-benefits-optimization

10 Common Insurance Mistakes to Avoid | Global Credit Union. (n.d.). Www.globalcu.org. https://www.globalcu.org/learn/insurance-tips/10-common-insurance-mistakes-to-avoid/

3 factors to help determine how much life insurance you need | F&G. (n.d.). Blog.fglife.com. Retrieved July 21, 2024, from https://blog.fglife.com/3-factors-to-help-determine-how-much-life-insurance-you-need

Beattie, A. (2023, July 19). *How Much Life Insurance Should You Carry?* Investopedia. https://www.investopedia.com/articles/pf/06/insureneeds.asp

Compare Car Insurance Rates & Shop Quotes Online (September 2023). (n.d.). MarketWatch. https://www.marketwatch.com/guides/insurance-services/compare-car-insurance/

Chen, J. (2021, June 17). *The Ups and Downs of Insurance Coverage*. Investopedia. https://www.investopedia.com/terms/i/insurance-coverage.asp

How to avoid these 5 mistakes when purchasing life insurance | MassMutual. (2021). Massmutual.com. https://blog.massmutual.com/insurance/life-insurance-tips

Insurance In Risk Management: 5 Things To Know. (2024, March 8). Resolver. https://www.resolver.com/blog/insurance-in-risk-management-new-businesses/

McMaken, L. (2019). *4 Types Of Insurance Everyone Needs*. Investopedia. https://www.investopedia.com/financial-edge/0212/4-types-of-insurance-everyone-needs.aspx

Metz, J. (2020, May 13). *Compare Car Insurance Quotes*. Forbes Advisor. https://www.forbes.com/advisor/car-insurance/car-insurance-quotes/

The Ultimate Guide for Choosing the Best Type of Life Insurance Policy | The American College of Financial Services. (n.d.). Www.theamericancollege.edu. https://www.theamericancollege.edu/knowledge-hub/insights/the-ultimate-guide-for-choosing-the-best-type-of-life-insurance-policy

Compounding Dividends: The Secret Sauce to Growing Your Portfolio. (n.d.). FasterCapital. Retrieved July 21, 2024, from https://fastercapital.com/content/Compounding-Dividends--The-Secret-Sauce-to-Growing-Your-Portfolio.html

Compound Interest: Long-Term Investing Strategies for Financial Growth. (2024, April 8). Bookmap. https://bookmap.com/blog/compound-interest-long-term-investing-strategies-for-financial-growth/

Estate planning: The Importance of Legacy Planning in Estate Management. (n.d.). FasterCapital. Retrieved July 21, 2024, from https://fastercapital.com/content/Estate-planning--The-Importance-of-Legacy-Planning-in-Estate-Management.html

Grimm, M. (2024, May 10). *Staying Sharp to Stay Ahead: Why Continuous Learning is Crucial as a Financial Advisor.* C2P Enterprises. https://c2penterprises.com/blog/staying-sharp-to-stay-ahead-why-continuous-learning-is-crucial-as-a-financial-advisor/

Investing 101. (n.d.). The Department of Financial Protection and Innovation. Retrieved July 21, 2024, from https://dfpi.ca.gov/investing101/

Legacy planning: Preserving Wealth in the Payout Phase. (n.d.). FasterCapital. Retrieved July 21, 2024, from https://fastercapital.com/content/Legacy-planning--Preserving-Wealth-in-the-Payout-Phase.html

Management, D. C. (2024, January 22). *The Power of Continuous Learning: Staying Informed in a Dynamic Market.* Davidsoncap.com. https://davidsoncap.com/the-power-of-continuous-learning-staying-informed-in-a-dynamic-market/

Roberts, W. C. (2006, January 1). *The Physician's Guide to Investing: A Practical Approach to Building Wealth by Robert M. Doroghazi, MD, FACC, with consulting editor Dan W. French, PhD.* Proceedings

(Baylor University. Medical Center). https://www.ncbi.nlm.nih.gov/pmc/articles/PMC1325290/

The Power of Compound Interest: Secrets to Long-Term Wealth Building. (2024). Nasdaq.com. https://www.nasdaq.com/articles/the-power-of-compound-interest:-secrets-to-long-term-wealth-building

Understanding compound interest can help you grow wealth. (n.d.). Fortune Recommends. https://fortune.com/recommends/banking/what-is-compound-interest/

Alex Knight

www.ingramcontent.com/pod-product-compliance
Lightning Source LLC
Chambersburg PA
CBHW031618210526
45464CB00004B/1634